University of Birmingham

URBAN AND REGIONAL STUDIES NO 4

I   The Social Framework of Planning

University of Birmingham

URBAN AND REGIONAL STUDIES

Problems of an Urban Society

VOLUME I

The Social Framework of Planning

J. B. CULLINGWORTH

LONDON · GEORGE ALLEN & UNWIN LTD
Ruskin House   Museum Street

ISBN 0 04 352044 8 hardback
     0 04 352045 6 paperback

Made and printed in Great Britain
in 10 point Times New Roman
by William Clowes & Sons, Limited
London, Beccles and Colchester

Preface

I owe a large debt of gratitude to the many friends who have helped me in the writing and editing of this work. The major debt is to my former colleagues—staff and students—in the Centre for Urban and Regional Studies at the University of Birmingham. No less valued have been the comments made by friends in local and central government. Consensus has not been achieved, nor attempted, and any shortcomings are entirely my own responsibility. In particular, it has proved impossible for me to bring all the chapters up to the same date. That the various chapters in Volumes I and II were written at different times during the academic year 1971–2 will be all too apparent. I am also extremely grateful to my diligent secretary, Mrs Gill King, who battled most efficiently with badly written drafts.

J.B.C.

Contents

Tables

Summary of Contents of Volumes II and III

Introduction

Few areas of debate have burgeoned in recent years as much as those concerned with urban problems. The reasons stem only in part from the growth of problems of urban decay, pollution, poverty, regional decline and the like. Of equal, if not greater importance are changing attitudes, changes in public awareness and in the limits of public toleration. As the complexities and interdependencies of modern life have increased, so has the resolve to combat the environmental and social ills to which these give rise. Concern for the quality of the environment is no longer the preserve of an intellectual minority of visionaries, administrators and politicians: it is a matter of concern to an electorate which is demanding greater 'citizen-participation' and more effective control over the vast and amorphous managerial institutions of contemporary society. At the same time, the threshold of tolerability has changed. The number of the homeless and the destitute is certainly less now than it was a century or even a generation ago, but it is not the statistics which are currently 'shocking': it is the fact that homelessness and destitution exist at all which has become intolerable. Of course, 'standards' have risen and concepts of poverty have changed beyond the wildest dreams of nineteenth century reformers. But this is irrelevant: each generation has to define for itself the criteria against which poverty is to be judged. Similarly with the physical environment: that towns are now relatively healthy places in which to live is a statistical fact, but this is of little relevance in the context of contemporary concern for the quality of the urban environment.

The point should not, however, be overstressed. The festering sores of slumdom still exist in some major cities and these bear a tragic resemblance to those described at length in the blue books of the nineteenth century. Further, they are hidden from—or, at least, are unseen by—the middle class commuter and, therefore, do not shock the public conscience or precipitate the necessary public action. There are no longer cholera epidemics to overcome ignorance of the conditions that exist. At the same time individualistic moral philosophy has been given a modern twist with the perceived (yet

15

unrealized) advent of 'the welfare state' and the defensive mechanisms rapidly and eloquently brought into play by the institutions of social welfare whenever major criticisms are made of their adequacy by social commentators. Curiously—and dangerously—the criticism of public and social service has become institutionalized to such an extent that 'direct action' is increasingly seen by some as being the only route to a change in 'the system'. At present the balance is heavily in favour of legitimized change within the system: by reform of institutional procedures, by consultative councils, by ombudsmen and, less surely, by neighbourhood groups. New styles of local government and new divisions of power are under serious discussion. Though there is a clear trend towards agreement on the need for large local authorities able to command substantial resources, responsible for meaningful areas of community interest, and capable of accepting a substantial devolution of power from central government, there is also a widely accepted need for truly local institutions able to express neighbourhood feelings and to undertake direct responsibility for matters which are of only local concern. The main debate, however, is surefooted only in the former field where the issues are clear (though difficult to evaluate and balance one against the other): so far as 'community councils' (to use the term employed in the new legislation on local government) are concerned, the debate has barely progressed beyond recognition of the need.

Reference is made throughout these three volumes to these and similar issues relating to the distribution of power, and an attempt is made, in the last chapter of Volume II, to draw the threads together, but the main purpose is less ambitious; it is to provide an outline of some of the major urban problems of contemporary Britain. The qualifying 'some' is essential, both because of the competence of the author to discuss all the relevant issues and also because the field is limitless. The majority of the population live in urban areas. What then should be the criterion by which some issues are included as 'urban and regional problems', while others are excluded? There is no easy answer to this and no claim is made that this book demonstrates one. The 'solution' is personal but, hopefully, not idiosyncratic. The intention has been to provide an introduction to those issues which, on one view, are among the more important.

The three volumes complement *Town and Country Planning in Britain* which gives an outline of the apparatus of physical planning but their focus is on problems and on social and (to a lesser extent) economic aspects. Some degree of overlap between the two works has been inevitable while, on the other hand, attempts to avoid this

16

have led to a rather more slender treatment of some issues (such as 'amenity') than might have been expected.

A common thread throughout is the inter-connectedness of issues. This presents a perpetual—and probably insoluble—problem for government, which must divide its responsibilities into manageable parts. A similar problem faces an author who attempts to provide a broad picture of the issues, even when the field is narrower and, within that field, comprehensiveness is explicitly disclaimed. To illustrate: should the transport problems of elderly people be dealt with in a discussion of transport or in a discussion of the elderly? Should issues relating to the size and composition of the labour force come under the heading of 'demography' or 'economics'? Is it more appropriate to deal with housing subsidies in the context of housing or that of poverty?

In practice the solution adopted matters less than the awareness that there are always different, and possibly equally relevant, contexts for each aspect of a many-sided issue. What is totally inadequate is to approach a 'problem' in the terms of a discipline or a profession. Economics, sociology and, indeed, all the separate social sciences are abstractions which deal with parts of problems defined by the nature of their analytical tools. In a similar way, professions deal with parts of problems defined by the nature of their corpus of knowledge and their operational skills; and government departments and ministers deal with parts of problems defined by the nature of the responsibilities which have been allocated to them.

The development of multi-disciplinary studies, of generic professions and of non-departmental offices are all attempts to break down these artificial barriers. These three volumes are offered as a modest contribution to the same endeavour.

The intention in dividing this work into three volumes was simple and logical. Volume I would set the framework within which specific problems could be discussed in Volume II. Volume III would then provide a set of complementary readings. As with all good plans, implementation proved less simple. The subject matter refused to be so neatly packaged. Where does the 'framework' end and the 'problem' begin? By the time the plan had been finalized it no longer seemed to have the validity which it had at conception. Nevertheless, the underlying concept of a three volume series spanning major contemporary urban problems remained.

Volume I: The Social Framework of Planning

In this first volume there is a general discussion of the demographic socio-economic and physical framework of 'planning', together with an account of the problems of urban traffic and a note on the land values problem.

The starting point is the size and structure of the population, recent demographic trends and their implications. This is prefaced by a short discussion on the concept of an 'optimum' population. The fact that this is elusive and difficult does not detract from its importance. Recognition of this has developed markedly in the twelve months since the first draft was written.

Demographic analysis rapidly becomes indigestible, and no attempt is made to achieve a comprehensive coverage. The aim is to provide sufficient to demonstrate some of the more important implications of current trends. The chapter includes, as a 'case study', some detailed figures on the South East Region: chosen mainly because of the wealth of available material on this Region.

The second chapter, on the socio-economic framework, deals in the main with employment, regional problems and policies, and urban growth policy. Again the concept of the 'optimum' is introduced, this time in relation to towns. But while the idea of an optimum population is viewed sympathetically, that of an optimum size of towns is severely criticized, particularly in view of the fact that controls over the growth of towns have formed a major plank of British planning policy, frequently with unintended and undesirable effects.

There is, of course, a clash here between a number of different objectives. This is more clearly seen in Chapter 3 which presents an even more selective treatment of the physical framework of planning problems and policies. The selected issues include urban growth, agriculture, forestry, water and natural resources. Since this chapter was drafted an important official study has been published on *Long Term Population Distribution in Great Britain*. An Appendix to Chapter 3 reproduces some of the main findings of this study. (A summary of the Report is reproduced in Volume III.)

Chapter 4 discusses urban traffic problems. This leans heavily (though by no means uncritically) on the writings of Professor Colin Buchanan. Emphasis is laid on environmental issues, road pricing and the development of public transport. Public support for these is currently growing. Unfortunately, no viable system of pricing has yet been devised and policy is therefore constrained to the narrower issue of parking controls.

Finally, a note is provided on the land values problem. This was forced to the fore of public debate just after the appropriate machinery for coping with it (the Land Commission) had been abolished. Though there is some reference to the immediately current problem, the main emphasis of the Chapter is on the broader issues. As with the majority of the problems discussed, practicable solutions depend upon public understanding and political leadership. The two schemes introduced by Labour Governments (in 1947 and 1967) failed politically and it is not easy to be hopeful that a third attempt will provide a long-term solution. Nevertheless there are, again, signs of changes in public opinion.

Volume II: The Social Content of Planning

Much of the second volume is concerned with urban poverty and disadvantage: the relative lack of command over resources and access to opportunity and power. Chapter 1 provides a review of the dimensions of poverty and serves as an introduction to the fuller discussion of selected issues in the chapters that follow.

Chapter 2 discusses the nature of housing policies, the special characteristics of housing and a number of issues relating to tenure and choice. The issue of 'choice' emerges more clearly in the chapter on slum clearance and improvement. In both chapters, the differences between the institutional frameworks of 'public' and 'private' housing are underlined. Unfortunately, though justified in historical terms, these differences now create additional 'housing' problems which are further exacerbated by political approaches to 'council housing' and 'owner-occupation'.

Chapter 4, on 'race and colour', is a documentation of the emergence and recognition of a new urban problem which has its roots in human prejudice and fear. Government is here faced with a series of difficult and delicate political problems. The problems are complicated by the fact that they are inextricably intertwined with wider issues of social justice and equality.

The 'colour problem' has resulted in a greater awareness of the social objectives and social implications of physical planning policies. This forms the subject of an extended discussion, in Chapter 5, of the nature and scope of 'social planning'. Increasingly, however, it is being recognized that 'the social' is but a label for one aspect of planning, in the same way that 'the physical' or 'the economic' are labels for other aspects.

Throughout these chapters there is repeated references to issues such as citizen participation, the distribution of power, and the essentially political nature of all 'planning'. The final chapter attempts a broad review of these issues and stresses the crucial importance of the political process. 'Planning' is essentially, not the

19

fufilment of plans, but a process of balancing conflicting claims on scarce resources and of achieving compromise between conflicting interests.

Volume III: Planning for Change

The third volume is intended not only to complement the first two volumes, but also to bring together a number of important papers on some crucial contemporary urban problems. The major theme is set out at length in Professor Mel Webber's challenging paper which lends its title (in abbreviated form) to the volume as a whole: what are the possibilities, the scope and the content of planning in a rapidly changing society? Some authors are more sure of themselves than others, though most raise more questions than can be answered.

The widespread interest raised by Webber's paper (originally delivered to the Bartlett Society and later printed in the *Town Planning Review*) is a result not only of the cogency of his argument and the felicity of his presentation, but also its particular timeliness. The 1960s saw the increasing rejection of deterministic, detailed 'development' planning and the increasing acceptance of flexible 'structure' planning. The impact was greater on thinking than on practice, but the new thinking underlay the planning legislation which was passed at the end of the decade. Moreover, Webber's 'permissive planning' approach was explicitly adopted in *The Plan for Milton Keynes* (to which Webber personally contributed).

The wider view of 'planning' has led to the creation of inter-disciplinary planning teams. Professor Alonso, in the second paper in this volume, questions the adequacy of these. He sees the inter-disciplinary team primarily as a source of innovation or dissent where new departures are called for. A new approach ('beyond the inter-disciplinary approach') is needed, in which urban and regional problems are dealt with by professionals who are first and foremost specialists in these problems and only secondarily members of traditional disciplines. This 'meta-disciplinary' approach is essentially problem-orientated—a point which arises again in the final paper of this volume.

The paper by Professor Donnison and his colleagues at the Centre for Environmental Studies, though focused on the Greater London Development Plan, demonstrates the inter-connectedness of urban problems and the way difficulties in solving them are exacerbated by definitions of areas of administrative and political responsibility.

This paper was submitted to the Greater London Development

Plan Inquiry in November 1970, and has not previously been published.

One of the points raised at the end of this paper is the difficulty facing the public in participating in the debate on the Greater London Development Plan. Yet public participation is now supposedly part of the planning process. The Skeffington Committee dealt specifically with this issue. Its Report, *People and Planning*, is the subject of further analysis in the fourth paper, by Levin and Donnison. The Report is shown to be only the beginning of an important debate, but though a number of proposals are put forward, Levin and Donnison necessarily conclude with more questions than answers.

With Peter Willmott's paper, modestly entitled 'Some Social Trends', we return to a theme touched upon in the second chapter of the first volume: the changing socio-economic framework. This broad review of social change in Britain argues that strong social forces are at work leading to a more homogeneous life-style.

A major element in current social change is demographic. Chapter 6 reproduces a short extract from the Crowther Report *15 to 18* which discusses demographic trends in the context of their educational consequences.

Much of the debate in the sixties was preoccupied with the problems of affluence, but each generation apparently has to 'rediscover' poverty. Adrian Sinfield's succinct paper (which extends the discussion contained in Chapter 1 of Volume II) reviews the state of knowledge on, and the awareness of, poverty in Britain. Originally published in 1968, its extensive bibliography has been up-dated.

Michael Thomson's paper on traffic provides a survey of the problems of a society which is about half way to the 'saturation level' of around one car to every two people. The title is deliberately tendentious since it is argued that a fully 'motorized' society is neither possible nor, indeed, desirable.

The study which is summarized in Chapter 11 (*Long Term Population Distribution in Great Britain*) is perhaps the most important review since the Barlow Report. The fact that it was carried out by civil servants (rather than a committee of inquiry or a Royal Commission) affects the style, but not the message. In essence this is that the scope for government intervention, control and direction is limited. As with Webber the emphasis is on the need for flexibility. However, there remains a large area for political debate here, which an expansion of research effort could render more profitable.

Research is the subject of the final chapter which reproduces, without amendment, the editor's Inaugural Lecture at the University

21

of Birmingham. This suffers from its brevity but, following the publication of, and debate on, the Rothschild and Dainton Reports (in *A Framework for Government Research and Development*, HMSO, 1971) it has an unexpected topicality. 'Planning for Change', if it is to be relevant and effective, demands a strong research base. But, as the paper argues, research workers must be wary of over-enthusiastic politicians. Research can provide information, understanding and advice, but the responsibility for decision making rests with politicians.

Chapter 1

The Demographic Framework

AN 'OPTIMUM' POPULATION SIZE

As many people may have to be accommodated in Britain in the final
third of this century as have been accommodated in the first two-
thirds. To some this constitutes a nightmare, but the great majority
of official witnesses who gave evidence to the Select Committee on
the consequences of population growth [1] took a complacent view.
The then Secretary of State for Local Government and Regional
Planning (Mr Anthony Crosland) voiced a common opinion: 'I have
not as yet heard any argument in terms of pressure on land which
leads me to the view that any government at the moment should have
an active population policy . . . proper and effective planning [can]
cope with the increased demand for space without any decline in the
quality of life.' A minority, however, like the Conservation Society,[2]
expressed serious concern about the increasing pressures upon the
limited land of Britain, and argued that 'additional numbers can
only diminish the quality of life'. The Select Committee echoed the
mounting public concern—of which its report was symptomatic—
and recommended the establishment, as an integral and permanent
part of the machinery of government, of a Special Office directly
responsible to the Prime Minister, which would study, appraise,
publicize and advise upon the implications of population trends.
Unfortunately, the report coincided with a major move (introduced
by the Conservative Government which was returned to power in
June 1970) to bring about 'less government, and better government,
carried out by fewer people'.[3] The time was, therefore, hardly
propitious for the setting up of a new piece of governmental machinery, particularly in such a politically delicate field. Nevertheless, it
was decided to appoint a 'small mixed panel of experts' to assess the
available evidence about the significance of population trends and to
identify the gaps in knowledge.[4]

For a complex of reasons, including the impossibility of predicting
the future and the difficulty of achieving consensus on the elements
which make up 'the quality of life', government has traditionally
steered clear of 'population policy'. This is in spite of the fact that a

Royal Commission on Population, which was set up in 1944 (following the large fall in births in the thirties), stressed that 'it is impossible for policy, in its effects as distinct from its intentions, to be "neutral" on this matter since over a wide range of affairs policy and administration have a continuous influence on the trend of family size'.[5] However, the problem arises in establishing direct causal relationships and in judging what an 'optimum' population size would be. Even if agreement could be reached on this, it would, in the words of the then Secretary of State for Social Services (Mr R. H. Crossman), 'be a terrifying prospect to know what one would do about it'. This is a field in which politicians have shown an untypical modesty. The power of government to influence events is frequently much less than they would have us believe: it is unusual to find them claiming, almost unanimously, that a crucial issue is beyond their powers, even though other countries have made the attempt with signally little effect.

There is no doubt that the issue is extraordinarily complex, but then so is economic policy—and who in the 1930s would have dreamt of an all-party commitment to full employment? The truth of the matter is that population policies would necessarily be very long-term both in their aims and their effects, and that short-lived governments are unlikely to attempt to influence such distant events unless they are compelled to do so by public opinion. There are signs that this may come. Though, as the experts stress, it may be impossible to determine the 'optimum' size of the population, public opinion may come to view the prospect of a major increase with such apprehension that government will be forced to act.

The scope for action and its likely effectiveness or otherwise cannot be explored here.[6] Our predominant concern is with the distribution of population over the country and the social and economic implications of its structure and its activities. Nevertheless, the starting point must be the size and growth of the population. The discussion will incidentally demonstrate some of the difficulties which would face the framers of a population policy.

TWENTIETH CENTURY POPULATION TRENDS

The population of the United Kingdom increased by 17 million between 1901 and 1971: from 38·2 million to 55·3 million. The major reason for this increase has been the excess of births over deaths, but outward migration reduced the total increase by some 2 million. The 1930s were exceptional in that there was a gain in population due to migration (averaging 90,000 a year): this was due to the influx of

THE DEMOGRAPHIC FRAMEWORK

European refugees and the fall in the number of British emigrants to the old Commonwealth in the economic depression of this period. The late fifties and early sixties were similarly exceptional: in this case because of immigration from the New Commonwealth. This was severely cut back by the 1962 Commonwealth Immigrants Act: since then there has been a net outflow of population.

The excess of births over deaths—the 'natural increase'—was at its highest in the first decade of the century, but the number of births declined greatly in the period up to the second war: from an annual average of 1,091,000 in 1910–11 to 720,000 in 1931–41. This gave rise to considerable anxiety, since though the population was still increasing, the number of births was insufficient to replace the generation to which their parents belonged. Had fertility remained at the low level of the thirties, the population would have declined in the long run. Indeed, there was speculation that the population might decline to 10 millions within a century.

A Royal Commission on Population set up in 1944 deliberated for five years and provided a sober assessment of the position, and concluded that total numbers would continue to grow, 'perhaps for another generation', but the growth would be neither rapid nor large. Future births would 'almost certainly' decline in the following fifteen years, but the more distant future could not be readily forecast. Nevertheless, if average family size remained constant, total numbers would reach a maximum around 1977 and would, thereafter, begin a slow decline. A small increase in family size would lead to a stabilization of the population—which the Commission thought to be eminently desirable. Though it was possible to hold widely different views about the optimum size of the population in relation to national resources, 'if over a long period parents have families too small to replace themselves, the community must undergo a slow process of weakening'.

It needs to be remembered that it was in this context that post-war planning was conceived. No one anticipated the very large and sustained growth which actually took place.

The nature of this change can be quickly outlined. Following the end of the war, an expected 'baby-boom' took place (as it did after the first war) and births rose rapidly to a peak of 1,025,000 in 1947. Thereafter, the number of births began to fall and the evidence appeared to point overwhelmingly to a reassertion of the low fertility pattern of the thirties. But the fall was arrested: in the mid fifties births averaged 800,000; by 1960 they topped 900,000; and in 1964 reached 1,015,000. (Since then they have fallen steadily, reaching 903,000 in 1970.) The Royal Commission had thought that 54 million was the highest likely figure for the population of the U.K. by the end of the century: this number was surpassed in 1966.

It is, however, one matter to present the figures: it is quite another matter to attempt an explanation. It is now widely believed that the prolonged economic depression of the thirties exerted a significant influence on the birth rate even though the currently used techniques of birth control were relatively inefficient. On this interpretation, post-war prosperity is a major factor. In fact, there are many threads here which are difficult if not impossible to untangle. During the inter-war years the sex-ratio at the normal marrying ages was considerably affected by the male slaughter which took place in the 1914–18 war: enforced spinsterhood was more than a newspaper story. Social attitudes have changed radically.[7] In 'the permissive society', the interval between meeting and marrying has shortened (and, lest this should be thought to be confined to the young, it needs to be pointed out that the interval has become proportionately even shorter for older women). Further, two-fifths of the first births to brides under the age of twenty at marriage are extra-maritally conceived (the proportion for the oldest brides—those whose age at marriage is forty or more—is also at the high rate of nearly 28 per cent).

Table 1   *Population of the United Kingdom, 1901–1971* [8]

	Population in millions				
	1901	1931	1951	1961	1971
England and Wales	32·5	40·0	43·8	46·1	48·6
Scotland	4·5	4·8	5·1	5·2	5·2
N. Ireland	1·2	1·2	1·4	1·4	1·5
United Kingdom	38·2	46·0	50·2	52·7	55·3

Whatever the underlying forces, the demographic features are clear. There has been a major increase in the popularity of marriage: more now marry and the age of marriage has fallen. In 1931, 26 per cent of women aged 20–24 had married, but in 1961 the proportion had risen to 57 per cent. The proportion ever-married in the age group 40–44 rose from 81 per cent in 1931 to 90 per cent in 1961. (It has since risen to 92 per cent.) The average age of women at first marriage was 25·7 in 1951 but 23·2 in 1961 (and 22·7 in 1968). Furthermore, though it is still a matter for conjecture, it is possible that the average number of live-born children to those marrying in the late fifties and early sixties will be nearly 2·5. (Currently, to achieve replacement the figure would need to be around 2·1.) This apparent

26

Table 2 *Elements of Population Change, Selected Periods* [9]

	Population in thousands				
	1901/11	1931/51	1951/56	1961/66	1968/69
De facto population at start of period	38,237	46,038	50,290	52,816	55,283
Average annual change:					
Live births	1,091	785	797	988	941
Deaths	624	598*	583	633	646
Net natural increase	467	188	214	355	295
Net civilian migration	−82	+22	−48	+12	−43
Net changes from deployment of armed forces between U.K. and elsewhere			+13	+1	−1
Overall increase	385	213	179	368	251

* Including deaths of non-civilians and merchant seamen who died outside the country.

trend does not signal a return to large families: it is explained by a substantial reduction in childlessness and by a shift from the one-child family to families of two or three children.

The moralist will also point to the increase in illegitimacy, from between 4 and 5 per cent of total births from 1890 to 1959, to 5·2 per cent in 1960, 7·3 per cent in 1965 and 8·3 per cent in 1969. This increase has roughly coincided in time with the trend to marriage at younger ages. (About a third of illegitimate births—now numbering 78,000 a year—are registered on 'the joint information of both parents', i.e. they have a legally recorded paternity.)

It is tempting to go further into this fascinating field of social arithmetic, but sufficient has been said for present purposes to illustrate the dramatic changes which have occurred over a short space of time. Prediction in this area is fraught with obvious difficulties: even more so than in the past. The spread of effective family planning (a further increase in which can confidently be predicted) results in a situation of 'quasi fertility control'. The control is operated by families themselves (though over a sixth of births are still 'accidental'—which is not, of course, the same as 'unwanted'), and thus social attitudes become a predominant factor in birth trends. Which way these attitudes will work in the future is a matter of speculation.

In this context of social change, population predictions are of limited value. The projections made by the Registrar Generals of the U.K. population in the year 2000 rose each year up to 1964 (when reached 74·7 million) but they have consistently fallen since then. As Professor D. V. Glass has so succinctly put it, 'there is no substitute for waiting'.

Nevertheless, it is long-term total population projections which are so difficult and subject to rapid change. (The projections for the year 2000 have dropped by two million each year since 1965.) Short-term total projections and long-term partial projections (relating to the population already born) are very much more reliable and, indeed, the most useful. This reliability is illustrated in Table 3, from which it is obvious that the variations are almost entirely in relation to children not born when the projection was made (to the left of and below the dotted line). The only significant exception is the 1964 projection of the over 35s, which was one million above the earlier—and the later—projection. This particular projection, unlike all the others, assumed a net *inward* migration: an assumption abandoned when control of Commonwealth immigrants was strengthened.

Thus projections of age-groups, for example over the age of twenty, can be safely made within narrow limits for a period of up to twenty years ahead. Indeed, for all services other than those involving children, projections of from fifteen to twenty years ahead are resonably reliable. Hence, the demographic elements which are

Table 3   *Estimated Total Population of the U.K. in 1990* [10]

Date of birth (mid-years)	Age in 1990	Population in millions—Projections of:				
		1955	1960	1964	1968	1969
Before 1955	Over 35	28·4	28·8	29·8	28·8	28·7
1955–1960	30–34	3·5	4·0	4·1	4·1	4·1
1960–1965	25–29	3·4	4·2	4·8	4·7	4·7
1965–1970	20–24	3·5	4·4	5·2	4·7	4·7
After 1970	Under 20	14·2	19·3	23·1	20·7	19·8
Total	All ages	53·1	60·6	67·0	63·2	62·0

The dashed line approximately divides those born before the projection was made (above the line) from those not then born.

relevant to housing need, the size of the labour force and retirement can all be predicted. Unfortunately, from the point of view of predictors, demographic elements are by no means the only relevant ones.

Table 4   *Age Structure of the Population of the U.K., 1941, 1969 and 1981* [11]

Age	1941	Millions 1969	Projected 1981
0–14	10·1	13·3	(14·1)
15–29	11·6	11·7	12·9
30–44	11·2	10·1	11·1
45–59	8·6	10·4	9·6
60–74	5·5	7·7	8·1
75 and over	1·3	2·5	3·0
	48·2	55·6	58·9
		Per cent	
0–14	21·0	23·9	(23·9)
15–29	24·0	21·1	22·0
30–44	23·3	18·1	18·9
45–59	17·8	18·6	16·4
60–74	11·3	13·8	13·7
75 and over	2·6	4·5	5·2
	100·0	100·0	100·0

The figures in brackets represent projections of those as yet unborn.

The Elderly

Unless there is some unexpected break-through in medical science, the future numbers of the elderly can be predicted with a high degree of accuracy. The number of people of retirement age increased by 97 per cent between 1911 and 1941, and by 54 per cent between 1941 and 1969. The 1969 projection for the year 2001 is for a relatively small increase of 9 per cent, though for those aged 85 and over it will be 60 per cent.[12]

As a proportion of the total population, those of retirement age constituted only 6·8 per cent in 1911, but 11·8 per cent in 1941, and 15·7 per cent in 1969. This is only in part a success of social policy: it is also due to the high birth rates at the turn of the century and the low birth rates of the inter-war years (which have reduced the proportion of the population in the 30–44 age group). Indeed, though the average life expectancy at birth has risen between 1901 and 1966 from 48·1 to 68·5 for males and 51·8 to 74·7 for females, for the over-60s it has increased by only two years for males (from 13·4 to 15·2) and by five years for females (from 14·9 to 19·7).[13] At the age of

29

70, the increase has been only one year for males and three years for females.

On current trends, though the number of elderly people will continue to increase until the eighties (from 8·6 million in 1968 to 9·7 million in 1981) there will be a fall thereafter (to 9·5 million in 2001). Whether there will be a fall in the *proportion* depends on future birth rates: on the 1969 projections the proportion would fall from 15·7 per cent in 1969 to 14·3 per cent in 2001. This must at present be unknown. (On the 1968 projection the proportion over retirement age in 2001 was 13·8 per cent: a significant difference from the projection made one year later.)

The elderly—like the other dependent age group (children)—make large calls on the social services, and they also have particular needs in relation, for example, to housing. Of special note is the growth of retirement areas, the demand for which may be expected to increase with a rising standard of living. At the other end of the economic spectrum, the elderly form a major part of the population living at or below the contemporary socially acceptable minimum standard.

Children

As has already been made abundantly clear, it is impossible to predict the number of children who may be born in the future. This is now a matter more under the direct control of the millions of parents than has ever previously been the case. The Victorian size of family has certainly gone, presumably for ever (if such a phrase can be used after so many dire warnings of the impossibility of prediction!). Of the couples marrying around 1860 over a half had six or more children, and a quarter had over eight. By contrast, for the marriages of 1925 only a quarter had four or more.[14] Average family size dropped for marriages of 1936 to 2·05 (below the replacement rate of roughly 2·1 live children per marriage). For the marriages of 1951 the estimated average is 2·23. The family sizes which will result from the marriages of recent years are not yet complete, but the average could possibly be 2·5.[15] A Government Social Survey inquiry[16] attempted to establish what a random sample of married women thought would be the size of their completed family and also the 'ideal' family size. This suggested that 2·5 children is regarded as being the desired level, and realistic in the sense that this is roughly what mothers expect, on average, to achieve. The 'ideal' in the sense of what parents would like to have if they had no financial problems is about 3·5 children per family.

Of all social groups, children make one of the largest claims on resources (or, to be more accurate, are accorded one of the largest shares of resources). They are, of course, a very large group, totalling (for those under 15) 13·2 million, thus considerably outnumbering the 8·6 million people over retirement age.[17] Their needs, unlike those of the elderly, cannot be delayed for long. There were nearly 2½ million more children in the schools of Britain in 1969 than there were in 1951.[18] More strikingly, over 6½ million new school places were provided between 1945 and 1970 at a cost of over £2,000 million.[19] Much of this building resulted from population movements, themselves frequently stimulated by the desire to provide better environment for children. (In the new towns alone, 456 new schools providing 231,000 places had been built by the end of 1971.)[20]

On current projections, the number of school children in Britain will rise by a further 2¼ million by 1985,[21] but once again we are into the area of unknown since these figures relate in part to children as yet unborn, and until they are born, there can be no certainty as to the numbers. Much more certain is the fact that before two decades have elapsed from the date of birth 'children' are into the housing market in very considerable numbers.

HOUSEHOLD FORMATION

The way in which a population is divided into separate households is of great importance to a number of issues, particularly housing. Obviously a population which consisted of households averaging five persons would need quite different numbers and types of houses than one of the same size which averaged two persons per household. This is by no means as far-fetched an illustration as might appear: between 1911 and 1966 the average size of household fell by a third, from 4·36 to 2·98 persons.[22] Had the 1966 population of England and Wales averaged the same household size as that of 1911 there would have been five million fewer households. The implications for housing, urban growth and land use are enormous.

The population in private households (i.e. excluding the 3 per cent in institutional accommodation) increased by 32 per cent from 1911 to 1966, but the number of households increased by 93 per cent. Even areas of population decline can have an increase in households.[23]

This increase in household formation is not solely a function of demographic change, important though this is. Analysis of this issue is helped by using the concept of *headship rates*.[24] A headship rate is simply the proportion of a given population group (e.g. married

31

males ages 30–34) who are heads of households. The concept can be applied either broadly, e.g. as in the 1951 Census Housing Report, where twelve groups were used, or in a greatly refined manner, as in the current work of the Department of the Environment, where 338 groups are used. (It goes without saying that the latter necessitates— and is made possible only by—the use of a computer.)

Headship rates vary greatly between different groups. Thus, while 97 per cent of married men aged 30–34 heading 'married couple families' were, in 1966, heads of households, the rate for single men of the same age forming single person households was 10·5 per cent, while for widowed and divorced men aged 50–54 heading 'lone-parent households' it was 38·6 per cent. Obviously, changes in age, marital condition and family circumstances can result—as they have done—in large changes in the number of households; but headship rates also allow an analysis to be made of how far non-demographic forces are at work.

Strangely, in spite of the intense interest in projecting future rates of household formation, little work has been done (or, at least, published) on changes in the past. A simple analysis undertaken by the author, however, showed that if headship rates had remained unchanged between 1951 and 1961, there would have been 600,000 fewer households at the latter date than were in fact recorded.[25] Unfortunately, the statistics which are currently published, though at a high level of sophistication, are impossible to manipulate in a simple manner. Whether the sophistication will permit accurate forecasts to be made of the number of future households remains to be seen.

Be that as it may, it is clear that there has been—and continues to be—a rapid increase in the proportion of the 'non-married' (i.e. the single, widowed and divorced) who form separate households. This cannot be accounted for solely on demographic grounds: it is in part a reflection of the improved standard of living. Increasing numbers of those who, at one time, would have lived with another household (either as part of an extensive family unit or as boarders) can now afford to live independently.

There is, however, a supply–demand relationship which, in this field as in many others, can confound projections. In an area where there is a high degree of 'sharing', changes in housing supply can significantly affect demand. This is important in relation to single people for whom the traditional types of accommodation are declining (at the same time as the number of 'independent single'—including students— is increasing). Bedsitters, 'flatlets', lodging and boarding accommodation are declining as a result of a number of factors. With a rising standard of living, fewer households with space to spare are willing to sub-let. Social security provisions and supplementary benefits work in the same direction, as may do controls over rents and multiple occupation. These factors may well act as a constraint on household formation by the single. An increase in supply (e.g. by housing associations) would remove the constraint.

Increasing mobility, and particularly movement to towns, is another factor in household formation. Surveys in several Swedish towns have shown that headship rates for the unmarried are far greater in urban than in rural areas.[26] They have also demonstrated that rates for the unmarried vary with the same age group according to income.

Many of these factors are at present imponderables. Much clearer is the situation in relation to the elderly. In 1966, a quarter of households in England and Wales consisted of one or two persons at least one of whom was of pensionable age—an increase of over half a million since 1961. The population of this age will certainly increase in the future and the proportion who will form separate households can be expected to increase also. Income maintenance and other social policies reinforce this trend. Of particular social significance is the trend away from institutional care, towards domiciliary support, for the elderly. There is great scope for (a somewhat unusual form of) household formation here. A Government Social Survey study led Amelia Harris [27] to an estimate that at least one in five of the residents of local authority residential homes 'need not have been given residential care if adequate housing could have been made available'. Miss Harris gives examples of elderly people whose tenancies lapse while they are in hospital; of those living 'with children whose own families are growing up and need their rooms, or who are in lodgings which they have to leave for one reason or another, and who find it difficult to get new lodgings, or who just cannot face the trial of trudging round trying to find somewhere else to live. There are, too, the "tied" tenants who find themselves homeless on retirement, as well as in a worsened financial position.'

Miss Harris stresses that her estimate is probably a minimum one:

It is noticeable that in many cases where the hospital or doctor advises residential care, the housing conditions are sub-standard. Hospitals are reluctant to discharge patients who come in with, say, bronchitis, to return to a damp house with an outside w.c., or a patient who has a heart attack or a fall to a couple of rooms at the top of a house with a coal-bunker and w.c. in the back yard. It is not unreasonable to assume that if adequate sheltered housing

PROBLEMS OF AN URBAN SOCIETY

were to be made available with supportive domiciliary services, some at least could avoid having to become residents.[28]

An increase in the supply of housing could not significantly affect the number of married couple separate households, for which the headship rate is already 98 per cent. (It should be stressed that the reference here is to the quantity of housing: qualitative factors are discussed in Chapter 2 of Volume II.) For the non-married and the elderly, however, a higher level of provision could significantly affect the situation.

Table 5   *Population and Households, England and Wales, 1911–1966*

	Population in private households		Households		Average household size
	Number (millions)	Average annual increase %	Number (millions)	Average annual increase %	Number of persons
1911	34·6	—	7·9	—	4·36
1931	38·0	0·5	10·2	1·5	3·72
1951	41·8	0·5	13·1	1·4	3·19
1961	44·5	0·6	14·6	1·2	3·04
1966	45·7	0·6	15·4	1·0	2·98
	No.	%	No.	%	%
Change 1911–1966	11·1	32	7·4	93	−32

HOUSEHOLD SIZE

It has already been noted that average household size has fallen dramatically during this century—in England and Wales, from 4·36 persons in 1911 to 2·98 in 1966. It is worth examining recent trends in a little more detail, if for no other reason than that when major trends of this kind take place scant attention is paid to the minority who do not 'conform' to them.

Between 1951 and 1966, the most spectacular change was a 68 per cent increase in one person households—from 1·4 million to 2·36 million. (In fact, because of underenumeration in the 1966 Census, particularly in relation to one person households, the real increase was somewhat greater than this.) Two person households also increased dramatically, by 29 per cent or rather more than one million. In numerical terms this was the largest increase of all. There were

34

more modest increases for households of four and five persons but, curiously, three person households fell in number between 1961 and 1966, to below the 1951 figure.

Larger households, of seven or more persons, had major percentage falls, but in absolute numbers the fall totalled only 69,000. While there were 457,000 households of seven or more persons in 1951, this figure had dropped only to 389,000 in 1966.

In short, while the increase in the numbers of one and two person households was huge, the fall in the numbers of large households was modest. About a half of these large households contained five or more dependent children: a group which is particularly at 'poverty risk'. This provides a corrective to the previous emphasis on the fall in average household size and the great increase in small households. There is a danger of a preoccupation with the needs of small households leading to inadequate concern for those of an 'abnormal' size: particularly in housing policy.

One final comment can be made in this short analysis of changes in household size: one which underlines the situation of the large household. Room-occupancy rates have traditionally been used as one measure of housing conditions. On this index, average conditions have improved enormously: the average number of persons per room fell from 0·74 in 1951 (0·83 in 1931) to 0·66 in 1961. A change in the definition of a room in 1966 (by which all kitchens were counted as rooms whereas previously they were ignored unless used for eating purposes) makes later comparison difficult,[29] but the fall certainly continued. Yet for many households of each individual size there was little change. In other words, the large fall in the overall position has resulted largely from the increase in small households living at low 'room-occupancy rates'.[30]

MIGRATION

Each year about 10 per cent of the population move. Most moves are made for housing reasons: only about one in six are due to job reasons.[31] Most moves are also over short distances: migration between regions constitutes only a small proportion of the total. Every area experiences movement within, into and out of its boundaries. This *gross* movement is on a vastly larger scale than the *net* change which results. For example, in the year preceding the 1966 Census, the West Midlands Conurbation had a net loss through migration of 9,080 people (representing 4 per cent of the 1966 population); but the *gross* movement was 278,580, made up of 187,120 people moving within the area, 41,190 moving into the area and

35

50,270 moving out of the area to other places in Great Britain. (This excludes those moving out of Great Britain, who obviously cannot be enumerated in a census of resident population.)

Over a five-year period the figures are, of course, very much higher (and they exclude multiple moves). On average, the rate of movement is about 33 per cent. In the West Midlands Conurbation, the let loss from migration between 1961 and 1966 was 41,900, but the gross movement (excluding multiple moves) was 889,000, made up of 592,620 people moving within the area, 127,240 into the area, and 169,140 moving out of the area to other places in Great Britain.

Even in the rapidly growing areas there is a considerable outward movement. Whiston Rural District in Lancashire, for example, into which 40 per cent of the 1966 population had moved since 1961, lost 8 per cent by outward migration during the same period. On a grand scale, Greater London gained 657,310 people and lost 826,380, resulting in a net migration loss of 169,070.

As these figures show, the cumulative effect of relatively small annual net change can be substantial. This is, of course, most striking in the case of small growing towns (Basingstoke doubled its population to 52,000 between 1966 and 1971), but can be significant in large old urban areas (the population of the Merseyside Conurbation fell from 1·38 million in 1966, to 1·26 million in 1971—a net fall of 120,000). These figures, however, include natural change. Since those who move tend to be younger than those who do not, there can be an important relationship between migration and natural change. This is most clearly seen in developing areas which attract young families at an early stage of the 'family cycle'. Population increase by migration is increased still further by rapid natural increase. Though it obviously does not appear in the statistics, the movement of young families results in a transfer of natural increase from one area to another. It follows that there is a tendency for migration to have a cumulative effect on population change: the 'exporting areas' lose not only their young but also their future children. Areas which lose populations over a long period will, therefore, tend to face a continuing decline and an 'ageing' of their population structure.

There are, however, other factors at work: for example, rates of natural increase vary between different regions even when age-structure is allowed for. Nevertheless, the cumulative changes for small communities and for inner urban areas can be dramatic.

In reviewing patterns of mobility an important concept is that of the 'family housing cycle'. The following passage taken from a report on a 1962 English housing survey,[32] though somewhat out of date in detail, is still in the main relevant. The first stage of a household's

36

(independent) history starts when the parental home is left on marriage or when a job is taken up in a new area. In this stage, households often live in small ill-equipped 'rooms' and 'converted flats'. Young people pay comparatively high prices for their accommodation.

The second stage in a household's 'housing history' begins with the birth of a first child. The 'small adult household' becomes a 'small family'. For those in rooms or 'flats' the shortcomings of the accommodation take on a new significance; more space is needed for storage and privacy; a separate bathroom becomes a necessity; a garden or some reasonably private outdoor space is needed. For those in older property the often cramped layout of the house and the street, together with the absence of a garden are similar constraints on the contemporary ideal of a home-centred family life. It is at this stage when mobility is greatest. A higher proportion now become owner-occupiers and (since they are now in recognized 'housing need') council house tenants. Incomes tend to be higher (though fewer housewives supplement the chief wage earner's income) and the average price of the house purchased rises. During this stage the family grows but, in spite of the high frequency of movement, overcrowding remains the principal problem for the group as a whole. As the children grow older, space becomes an acute problem, but the worst crowding comes to an end when the children reach marrying age (some before they are out of their teens) and split off to start their own independent housing history.

The final, and less clearly definable, stages of the housing cycle begin at different ages for different types of household. Grandparents, childless widows and elderly widowers lead very different lives and need different types of housing, but comfort, convenience and warmth become increasingly important for them. Though many of them have plenty of space—often too much—its very abundance poses problems for them. Some can, and do, let off part of their accommodation to households at the first housing stage, or to other old people, but the great value which is attached to independence and privacy prevents this from becoming significant. Despite their plentiful space it is at this stage that housing standards deteriorate sharply. For these are the people whose crucial housing decisions were made thirty or forty years ago, when the housing shortage was considerably more acute than it is today, when owner-occupation was less widespread and when council housing was still in its infancy. As a result, a large proportion of them now live in rented (frequently rent-controlled) property which is the poorest sector of the housing market. Their inclinations to move to better accommodation are tempered by a wish to retain the stability and familiarity afforded by the house and district which they have known for so long, and restrained by falling income and incapacity to borrow. For many the opportunities to move are considerably restricted.

To this needs to be added the important locational element. Young people are drawn into the central urban areas by the attractions of educational and economic opportunities. On marriage they may have to continue to live in the high cost inner urban housing market, but increased mobility and the operation of the institutions of the housing market (particularly building societies) may lead them to seek suburban locations. These become more attractive as the family grows. Rising real incomes and the inflation of house prices enables them at a later stage to move further out, possibly into commuter villages beyond the green belt. On retirement, they may move finally to a coastal area or an inland rural retirement area.

These two patterns of mobility are here presented in a highly capsulated manner. They are not at all points mutually consistent; nor can they be, since no such 'pattern' can fit all regions or all income groups. Nevertheless, they do represent two discernible trends which are of crucial importance to urban and regional planning, and we shall have cause to refer to them at various points in later chapters.

Strikingly absent from this account, however, is adequate reference to job opportunities. While it is true that the majority of moves are made for housing reasons, the minority which are made for job reasons are important. And it is obvious that areas of high economic activity will tend to attract labour from areas of low economic activity. Between 1961 and 1966 the central West Midlands, for instance, had an increase in employment of nine per cent and a net inward migration of seven per cent. By contrast, the central and eastern valleys of industrial South Wales had no net increase in employment during this period and experienced a net outward migration of 4 per cent.[33] However, net migration changes are, as already explained, a compound of much larger gross movements. Regions which lose by net migration tend to do so not because of extremely high rates of outward movement so much as because of low rates of inward movement.

This is reflected in the regional statistics of birthplace: in 1966, while 68 per cent of the population of the East Anglia and South West Regions, and 75 per cent of the South East Region were born in these regions, the proportion of native born Scots in Scotland totalled 92 per cent.

The cumulative effect of a net outward regional movement can be substantial, particularly when it is remembered that migrants take their natural increase with them. Thus, while England and Wales experienced an 11 per cent population increase between 1951 and 1971, East Anglia increased by 21 per cent whereas the North and Wales increased by only 5 per cent.

Regions cover very large areas and none have, as yet, experienced an actual decrease in population. Between 1961 and 1971, however, eight geographical counties had losses ranging from 0·5 per cent to 8·2 per cent. Six of these were in Wales and two in the north— Cumberland and Lancashire. London also lost 7·9 per cent of its population but this was a resultant of 'spill-over' into and beyond the green belt. What characterizes the population losses of the provincial counties is lack of economic growth leading to relatively long-distance migration.

Population losses from industrial towns are much more numerous. Fifty-eight towns with 1971 populations of 50,000 or more had lower populations in 1971 than in 1961. But at the level of the individual town it is important to distinguish between the effects of economic decline and of 'spill-over' into the surrounding countryside. Thus, the 18,100 population decline experienced by Portsmouth during 1961–71 is a very different matter from the 11,400 decline in Rhondda.

All migration statistics are affected by the boundaries of the areas to which they relate, and since the boundaries of local authorities have changed so little since the nineteenth century it is important to have regard to 'real' socio-economic areas. Nowhere is this more apparent than in Greater London, where the population of the present administrative area has fallen by 1¼ million since 1939. Nevertheless, since migrants tend to differ in important ways (e.g. age, social class and income) from non-migrants, 'spill-over' can have serious long-term implications particularly for administrative areas with obsolete boundaries.

International Migration

Historically, international migration has had a major impact on the growth of the population. Between 1815 and 1914 over 20 million people emigrated from Great Britain and Ireland (a large proportion, of course, from Ireland), of which 13 million went to the United States.[34] Had this massive emigration not taken place, the population would now be much larger than it is.

With the exception of the thirties and the period from the late fifties to early sixties, net emigration has been the rule. The latter period (following the 1952 McCarran-Walter Act which restricted migration from Jamaica to the United States, leaving Britain as the

39

PROBLEMS OF AN URBAN SOCIETY

only major industrial country open to large-scale migration from the West Indies[35]) saw the growth of West Indian immigration. In 1961, as the fear of controls developed, this increased and was accompanied by significant increases in immigration from India and Pakistan.[36] The controls introduced by the Commonwealth Immigrants Act of 1962 greatly reduced immigration and led to a reversion to the 'normal' situation of an excess of emigration over immigration (totalling 65,000 in 1966–67 and 20,000 in 1967–68). Cross flows are very much larger than net flows. In 1967–68, for example, the net emigration of 20,000 resulted from a gross immigration of 293,000 and a gross emigration of 312,000.

REGIONAL POPULATIONS

Throughout the nineteenth and twentieth centuries the populations of every region of Britain have continually grown,* but the rates of increase have varied both between regions and in different periods. Thus, the fastest growing region between 1801 and 1851 was the North West (with an increase of 186 per cent compared with a national rate of 98 per cent); between 1851 and 1901 it was the Northern Region (115 per cent; national 78 per cent); between 1901 and 1951 it was the West Midlands (48 per cent; national 32 per cent); and between 1951 and 1966 it was East Anglia (14 per cent; national 9 per cent).

The geographical distribution of the population in 1966 was the same as in 1801, but while there was a shift from the south to the north in the nineteenth century, this was reversed in the twentieth: a reflection of the decline of the old staple industries of the north, such as coal, shipbuilding and cotton, and the rise of modern light industries located in the south.

These broad trends mask important regional differences. The growth of population in Scotland, for example, has been consistently below the national average and its share of the national population fell from 15·3 per cent in 1801 to 12·1 per cent in 1901 and 9·8 per cent in 1966. East Anglia and the South West had relatively very low rates of growth in the nineteenth century and did not exceed the national average until the post-war period.

The major factor in these regional changes was migration. All the northern regions, Wales and Scotland experienced net losses by migration, while all the southern regions gained. Scotland stands out by virtue of the size of its migration loss: approaching half a million

* Except for Scotland in 1951–53 and 1964–66.

over the fifteen year period. (Between 1966 and 1970 net migration from Scotland totalled 124,000 of which 48,000 was overseas.[37]) Migration is, of course, closely related to the state of the regional economy, but it is not the only factor. Some of the growth in East Anglia and the South West is due to dispersal (mostly 'unplanned') from London. In the South West, retirement migration is substantial. Furthermore, net changes in certain regions have recently been accounted for wholly by immigration from overseas as distinct from inter-regional movement in Britain: this was the case during 1961–66 in the South East and the West Midlands. With the marked fall in immigration from overseas, both these Regions began to experience a net loss by migration.

Table 6   *Regional Population Changes, Great Britain, 1801–1966*

	Scotland, the North and Wales	Midlands and the South
Regional population growth as percentage of national		
1801–1851	113	90
1851–1901	111	91
1901–1951	71	127
1951–1966	49	141
Geographical distribution of population (%)		
1801	43	57
1851	46	54
1901	48	52
1951	44	56
1966	43	57

The importance of migration is abundantly clear. Nevertheless, with the one exception of the South West (where natural increase amounted to slightly less than half the total increase) the excess of births over deaths was the most important element in population growth during the period 1951–66. Furthermore, the range of regional variation in natural increase has been smaller (from 5·5 per cent in Wales to 10·9 per cent in the West Midlands) than for total change (from 1·7 per cent in Scotland to 14 per cent in East Anglia). Differences between regions in their natural increase are in part due to differences in their age structure (themselves strongly affected by migration history), and in part by traditional regional differences in fertility. Both Scotland and the Northern Region are areas of traditionally high fertility.

41

Table 7 *Regional Population Changes, 1951–1966*

	Population 1951		Natural change 1951–1966		Net migration 1951–1966	Natural change as % of total change 1951–1966	Population 1966		Total population increase 1951–1966 %
	No. (thousands)	*%*	*No. (thousands)*	*%*	*No. (thousands)*		*No. (thousands)*	*%*	
Northern	3,130	6·4	297	9·5	−116	159	3,317	6·2	6·0
Yorkshire & Humberside	4,488	9·2	331	7·4	−112	136	4,731	8·9	5·4
North West	6,417	13·1	425	6·6	−152	144	6,713	12·6	4·6
East Midlands	2,913	6·0	278	9·5	94	72	3,299	6·2	13·2
West Midlands	4,426	9·0	481	10·9	82	84	4,999	9·4	12·9
East Anglia	1,388	2·8	108	7·8	86	56	1,582	3·0	14·0
South East	15,216	31·1	1,215	8·0	542	68	17,006	32·0	11·8
South West	3,247	6·6	192	5·8	223	49	3,635	6·8	11·9
Wales	2,589	5·3	142	5·5	−39	127	2,701	5·1	4·5
Scotland	5,103	10·4	532	10·4	−478	602	5,194	9·8	1·7
Great Britain	48,917	100	3,326	8·2	608	96	53,176	100	8·7

SUB-REGIONS

Regions are, of course, very large areas within which there is great diversity. Sub-regional analysis, however, cannot be summarized here: it is sufficient to illustrate the types of trend which are observable at this level. Further illustrations, in relation to particular problems, are given in later chapters.

It has been indicated that, though (typically) natural increase is the most important factor in regional population change, migration is the factor which largely explains variations from national trends. This is true also at the sub-regional level, but here changes due to migration are far more dramatic: from a net gain (1951–66) of nearly a half in the eastern sector of the Outer Metropolitan Area to a net loss of 13 per cent in north east of Scotland. But migration also affects the age-composition of sub-regional populations (much more markedly than at the regional level) and subsequently the rate of natural increase. As a result a 'typology' of sub-regional areas can be devised.

The conurbations, for instance, have all experienced substantial net losses to their surrounding areas between 1951 and 1971, and as a group are experiencing an actual decline in population. In Clydeside, Tyneside, the West Midlands and the South East Lancashire Conurbations, this decline is fairly recent but the Greater London Conurbation has had a persistent decline for two decades. (Its population in 1971 was 7·4 million compared with 8·2 million in 1951.)

By contrast, the areas surrounding the conurbations have typically experienced major population increase due to high rates of net migration and associated natural increase.

The term 'surrounding' is, however, no longer appropriate in relation to London. The Outer Metropolitan area (which gained 1,129,800 people by migration between 1951 and 1968, in addition to a natural increase of 543,200) [38] began to lose population on balance by migration to more distant areas in and beyond the South East Region in the mid-sixties.

The loss of population from Greater London has now extended over the Metropolitan Region, with complementary gains to areas increasingly distant from London. This shift of population is now taking place over such a huge area as to affect regional trends (the South East Region as a whole—though growing by natural increase— had a small net loss of population by migration in 1965–6).*

The trend which is apparent in the London area, and mirrored in

* This excludes the gain caused by immigration from abroad.

43

the areas around the provincial conurbations, is to be observed also around other major urban centres. But around the older industrial areas the increases in the expanding commuter hinterland were less than the loss experienced by the urban areas. Thus, while all urban areas generally have expanded hinterlands, those of the north are characterized by a sub-regional migration loss whereas those of London and the West Midlands are characterized by a sub-regional migration gain. Nevertheless, no generalization of this type can be wholly valid and, as commuter areas develop further and further away from the urban areas, the picture becomes more and more complex.

Retirement migration adds to this complexity. In the South West this is on such a large scale that its impact is significant at the regional level. Retirement migration, however, is typically local in its impact, e.g. in the coastal areas of North Wales, the Fylde and Sussex. These are areas with a high proportion of elderly people and a natural decrease in population: retirement migration thus does not give rise to a very high rate of total population growth. But in 'newer' retirement areas (mostly rural) retirement migration is in some cases reversing a long-term population decline.

Remoter rural areas particularly in Scotland, Wales and Northern England, however, continue to experience both low rates of natural increase and high rates of outward migration; and, similarly, in the older industrial areas in these regions. As a result, between 1951 and 1971, the population of North East Lancashire fell by 4 per cent, and that of Central Wales by 8 per cent.

Between 1951 and 1966, the highest rates of net inward migration were to the eastern sector of the Outer Metropolitan Area (49 per cent), the coast of North Wales (20 per cent) and the areas to the north of the West Midlands Conurbation (18 per cent). In terms of total change the eastern sector of the Outer Metropolitan Area was the highest (64 per cent); areas with over 13 per cent increase included North Wiltshire (23 per cent), the coastal belt of industrial South Wales (18 per cent) and the Falkirk/Stirling area (14 per cent).

This rapid survey highlights three major types of migration: suburban—from urban areas to commuter hinterlands; economic—from more remote rural areas of northern Britain and from areas of economic decline to areas of economic growth; and retirement—from many areas to attractive coastal and rural areas. Figures for areas smaller than those of sub-regions would, of course, be more dramatic, but would be considerably affected by the arbitrary nature of local authority boundaries.

Ages of Migrants

Migrants do not form a cross-section of the population: they are typically younger and at an early stage of the 'family housing cycle'. This is true both of all migrants and of those who cross regional boundaries (and who are the subject of the present analysis). In 1965–66, some 700,000 people were involved in 'inter-regional flows' within Great Britain. Those in the 15–24 age group are the most mobile; next comes those aged 25–44, followed by the related children in the youngest age group (Table 8). The elderly are the least mobile, though their mobility may well be increasing.

Census data (which is not completely reliable) [39] shows that inter-regional migration increased between 1960–61 and 1965–66 (in absolute numbers, from 627,100 to 705,220). This increase was only in part due to changes in the size and age-structure of the population: about 80 per cent of it was due to increases in mobility (particularly prominent in the 25–44 age group).

It would be too complex a matter to detail all the inter-regional patterns, but in the following section the South East Region is taken as a case study in which this and other features of migration can be examined.

Table 8   *Age Structure of Inter-Regional Migrants, 1965–1966*

	No.	*%*	*Ratio of migrants to population*
1–14	169,520	24	1·50
15–24	181,540	26	2·40
25–44	231,550	33	1·77
45–59	64,600	9	0·64 ⎫ 0·63
60+	58,010	8	0·61 ⎭
All ages	705,220	100	

THE SOUTH EAST REGION: A CASE STUDY

The South East Region is the largest in terms of population (17·2 million: 31 per cent of the U.K. total) and, except for Scotland, also in terms of area (10,500 sq. miles: 11 per cent of the U.K. and 18 per cent of England and Wales). It is also the region on which the most comprehensive analyses have been produced.[40]

Between 1961 and 1966, the Census records 1,036,000 migrants into the South East and 929,000 out of the Region, giving a net migration increase of 107,000 (Table 9). This, however, was made up

of a net loss of 17,000 by inter-regional movement within Great
Britain and a net gain of 124,000 from elsewhere in the British Isles
and abroad. (These figures necessarily exclude emigration from
Britain, which is not recorded in the Census.)

The 'loss' to the rest of Great Britain was to only the adjoining
regions, particularly the South West and East Anglia, with a smaller
amount to the East Midlands. Further distant regions were, on
balance, a source of gain to the South East.

There are, thus, two quite distinct movements: a continuation of
the 'drift to the south' (though figures for 1965–66 suggest that this
was balanced at the end of the five-year period by movement north-
wards); and a major movement from the South East to adjacent
regions. This latter movement is the 'edge' of a major flow of movement from the inner parts of the Region: 234,000 from Greater
London to the Outer Metropolitan Area and 179,000 to the Outer
South East.

Also of particular importance to this Region is immigration from
overseas. Between 1961 and 1966 immigration into Great Britain
totalled 940,000, of which over a half settled in Greater London and
elsewhere in the South East.

Table 9   *Movement Into and Out of the South East Region,
1961–1966*

	In from	*Thousands* Out to	Balance
Adjoining regions			
East Anglia	44	82	−38
South West	112	165	−54
East Midlands	46	55	− 9
Total	203	303	−100
Rest of Great Britain			
West Midlands	67	55	+12
Wales	36	31	+ 5
North England	165	127	+38
Scotland	61	33	+28
Total	329	246	+83
Changes by inter-regional movement	532	549	−17
Rest of British Isles and abroad	504	380*	+124
Total migration change	1,036	929*	+107

* Does not include migration abroad.

An analysis of the age structure of migrants in the single year 1965–66 (Table 10) shows that the outward flow from Greater London is of all age groups, but the relative importance of each age group varies between different parts of the Region. The flow to the Outer South East suggests a strong retirement motivation: over a half of migrants are aged 45 and over. (Though not shown in the Table—which summarizes only the net balance—one third of migrants from Greater London to the Outer South East are aged 60 or over, while the opposite inflow has only one-fifth in this age-group.) By contrast, the flow from Greater London to the Outer Metropolitan Area is heavily concentrated in the younger working-age and related child groups.

Migration into, within and (increasingly) to adjoining regions is clearly of importance to the South East. Nevertheless, over the Region as a whole, natural change was three times as important over the years 1951–68 and over ten times as important in 1966–68, despite the increase in gross migration flows. (From 1966–68 the annual average natural increase was 102,600, while migration—plus the net effect of demobilization and recruitment and other changes in the distribution of the Armed Forces—was only 9,000.) But the position can be reversed for particular parts of a region. The huge migrational gain in the Outer Metropolitan Area from 1951 to 1968 (1,129,100) was twice as large as the natural increase over this period.

However, migration and natural increase interact. Thus, while net migration into the Outer Metropolitan Area was three times the rate of natural increase in the fifties, by the mid-sixties they were of similar order. This was partly the result of a lower rate of net migration but also a doubling of natural increase. A detailed statistical picture of the changes in the Region from 1951 to 1968 is given in Table 11.

Table 10   *Net Movement from Greater London to Other Parts of the South East by Age-Group, 1965–1966*

Age-group	To rest of South East		Of which:			
			To Outer Metropolitan Area		To Outer South East	
	No.	%	No.	%	No.	%
1–14	21,400	23	15,800	24	5,600	20
15–24	8,000	9	8,000	12	—	—
25–44	34,100	36	26,400	40	7,700	27
45+	30,200	32	15,000	23	15,200	53
All ages 1+	93,700	100	65,200	100	28,500	100

Population projections for regions are even more hazardous than national projections. The 1981 projection for the South East which was made in 1965 (18,970,000) was 552,000 greater than that made in 1967 (18,418,000). The South East Joint Planning Team's (SEJPT) fourteen projections for 1981 gave a range of variation of 2¼ million —from 17,607,000 to 19,884,000. It was with good reason that the Team concluded that 'since many of the assumptions change with the passage of time it becomes quite impossible to forecast population and employment levels with any certainty well into the future'.

Table 11   *Estimated Home Population Changes and Components of Change, South East Region, 1951–1968*

	South East Region	Greater London	Outer Metropolitan Region	Outer South East
Population	*(millions)*	*(millions)*	*(millions)*	*(millions)*
1951	15·22	8·21	3·51	3·50
1961	16·35	7·98	4·52	3·85
1966	17·01	7·84	5·01	4·17
1968	17·23	7·76	5·18	4·29
Percentage distribution				
1951	100·0	54·0	23·0	23·0
1961	100·0	48·8	27·6	23·5
1966	100·0	46·1	29·5	24·5
1968	100·0	45·1	30·1	24·9
Total change				
1951–61	1,129,100	− 228,500	1,011,900	345,900
1961–66	660,800	− 144,200	491,400	313,500
1966–68	223,300	− 72,400	169,700	125,800
1951–68	2,013,200	− 445,100	1,673,000	785,200
Annual average change: natural increase				
1951–61	66,400	33,300	24,200	8,900
1961–66	110,200	52,300	43,400	14,500
1966–68	102,600	46,300	42,300	14,000
1951–68	83,500	40,500	32,000	11,100
Annual average change: migration and balance				
1951–61	46,500	− 56,200	77,000	25,700
1961–66	21,900	− 81,200	54,900	48,200
1966–68	9,000	− 82,400	42,500	49,000
1951–68	34,900	− 66,600	66,400	35,000
Components of change, 1951–68				
Natural Increase	1,420,200	687,700	543,200	189,200
Migration and Balance	593,000	− 1,132,700	1,129,800	595,400
Total	2,013,200	− 445,100	1,673,000	785,200

A 'projected population' was abandoned in favour of a 'design population figure'.[41] The design figure for 1981 was 18·6 million; for 1991, 20 million, and for 2001, 21·5 million. Provision for some degree of flexibility was made by allowing for a possible further growth of 1½ million to the end of the century.

Even more problematic are projections for divisions of a region. This is nicely illustrated by the fact that the population envisaged for Greater London in 1981 by the Greater London Development Plan (and endorsed by the SEJPT) was virtually reached in 1971. The SEJPT figure for 1981 was 7,335,700, while the preliminary 1971 Census figure was 7,379,000. The assumption that the population of Greater London would fall annually by an average of around 34,000 proved very wrong: the annual fall averaged over 90,000—more than double the rate being experienced when the SEJPT was engaged on the Studies for the Strategic Plan.[42]

Regional and local population changes are the result of two types of factors: demographic and socio-economic forces not amenable to control, and such matters as land availability and the permitted density of development which is susceptible to far greater control. Between mid-1960 and mid-1967 the net outward movement from Greater London amounted to 496,000. Of this, 152,000 was 'planned movement to new and expanding towns', while 344,000 was 'voluntary movement'. In the fifties and early sixties most of this movement was to the Outer Metropolitan Area, but the restrictive policy being applied over much of this Area (which includes the green belt), together with increased planning provision for development in the Outer South East, implies an acceleration of the 'ripple' effect of waves of growth extending further and further from London. This has important implications for employment, journeys to work and a wide range of other socio-economic issues which are discussed at various points in later chapters.

One further implication of the impact of migration in this Region can be noted, though it should be stressed that no simple causal relationships exist: migration is only one of a complex of factors. Nevertheless, migration has been of major importance in household formation in the Region. In the Outer Metropolitan Area, 41·3 per cent of households in 1966 consisted of one or two persons. Further out—in the Outer South East, the proportion was 50 per cent. In Greater London, however, the proportion was again 50 per cent. (The national average in 1966 was 45·9 per cent.) The differences reflect the differing patterns of migration: the elderly to the Outer South East, married couples with children to the Outer Metropolitan Area and large numbers of young single people to Greater London.

This is a particularly striking illustration of the patterns of mobility outlined earlier.

The Greater London situation, especially in the inner area, is especially interesting. Not only does this area have a relatively high proportion of young single people: it also has high headship rates among this group. Nearly nine per cent of young single men in Inner London form one person households: more than double the proportion in any other planning sub-division of England and Wales.[43]

This short outline of some of the demographic features of the South East Region illustrates their importance in the framework of planning. (Other illustrative material can be found in the now substantial library of regional and sub-regional studies.) [44] The size and composition of the population is, however, only one aspect of this framework, and demographic factors are inextricably intertwined with a host of economic and social factors. A number of the more significant of these are discussed in the following chapter.

References and Further Reading

1. First Report from the Select Committee on Science and Technology, Session 1970–71, *Population of the United Kingdom*, H. C. Paper 379, May 1971. The Minutes of Evidence and Appendices of this Committee were published in May 1970, just before the dissolution of Parliament and the change of Government (H.C. 271, May 1970). The 1971 Paper reproduces all these in addition to the (reconstituted) Committee's Report and an updated memorandum on population growth.

2. The Conservation Society was founded in 1966 'in the belief that it was essential to tackle the basic causes of our environmental malaise'.

3. White Paper, *The Reorganisation of Central Government*, Cmnd. 4506, HMSO, 1970.

4. White Paper, Population of the United Kingdom, *Report from the Select Committee on Science and Technology: Observations by the Government*, Cmnd. 4748, HMSO, 1971.

5. Royal Commission on Population, *Report*, Cmd. 7695, HMSO, 1949.

6. See D. E. C. Eversley, 'The Special Case—Managing Human Population Growth', in L. R. Raylor (ed.), *The Optimum Population for Britain*, Academic Press, 1970.

7. The following section leans heavily on the evidence of Professor D. V. Glass to the Select Committee, op. cit., H.C. 379, 1971, p. 186 *et. seq.*

8. Census 1971, England and Wales, *Preliminary Report*, 1971, Table 2.

9. *Social Trends*, No. 1, 1970, Table 10.

10. Select Committee on Science and Technology, op. cit., p. 7.

11. J. Thompson, 'The Growth of Population to the End of the Century', *Social Trends*, No. 1, 1970, Table V.

12. Ibid.

13. *Social Trends*, No. 1, 1970, Table 59. The figures relate to Great Britain.

14. Royal Commission on Population, *Report*, Cmd. 7695, HMSO, 1949, Table XVII, p. 26.

15. Select Committee, op. cit., p. 4.

16. M. Woolf, *Family Intentions*, Office of Population Censuses and Surveys, HMSO, 1971. These results are viewed by some experts with considerable scepticism: see evidence of Professor D. V. Glass and Dr Bernard Benjamin, Select Committee, op. cit., Q.750–1 and 586.

17. 1968 figures (U.K.), Select Committee, op. cit., p. 9.

18. *Social Trends*, No. 1, 1970, Table 73. The figures were 1951: 6,891,000; 1969: 9,327,000.

19. *Annual Abstract of Statistics 1971*, Tables 102 and 108.

20. The figures relate to the period from the date of designation to December 1971, and are from *Town and Country Planning*, January 1972, p. 41.

21. *Social Trends*, No. 1, 1970, Table 74.

22. All figures relate to England and Wales only.

23. A fall of Greater London's population from 8·2 to 7·9 million was accompanied by an increase in households from 2,619,000 to 2,690,000. (1966 figure adjusted for under-enumeration.) Greater London Development Plan, *Report of Studies*, p. 15, Table 2.8.

24. For further discussion see A. H. Walkden, 'The Estimation of Future Numbers of Private Households in England and Wales', *Population Studies*, Vol. 15, No. 2, November 1961, pp. 174–183; J. B. Cullingworth, *Housing Needs and Planning Policy*, Routledge, 1960; and Ministry of Housing and Local Government, Statistics for Town and Country Planning, Series III: Population and Households, No. 1, *Projecting Growth Patterns in Regions*, MHLG, 1970.

25. J. B. Cullingworth, 'Housing Analysis', in S. C. Orr and J. B. Cullingworth, *Regional and Urban Studies: A Social Science Approach*, Allen & Unwin, 1969.

26. See Economic Commission for Europe, *Studies of Effective Demand for Housing*, United Nations, 1963.

27. Amelia I. Harris, *Social Welfare for the Elderly*, Government Social Survey, HMSO, 1968.

28. Ibid., p. 47. Miss Harris continued: 'Another indication that housing is a main factor affecting the use of residential accommodation is that a much higher proportion of elderly who were living as boarders, or in rooms or lodgings, became residents than would have been expected from the numbers of elderly living in these conditions. On the other hand, a much lower proportion of Local Authority tenants (most of whom are reasonably housed) have to be allocated residential places.'

29. For 1966, the change in definition resulted in a major decrease in the number of dwellings with four or less rooms and a corresponding increase in the number with five or more. See 1966 Census, *Great Britain Summary Tables*, HMSO, 1967, Table 16.

30. For further historical discussion see W. V. Hole and M. T. Pountney, *Trends in Population, Housing and Occupancy Rates, 1861–1961*, HMSO, 1971; J. B. Cullingworth, *Housing Needs and Planning Policy*, Routledge, 1960, Chapter 2; and 1931 Census, *Housing Report*, HMSO, 1935.

31. See, *inter alia*, D. V. Donnison, C. Cockburn and T. Corlett, *Housing Since the Rent Act*, Codicote Press, 1961; J. B. Cullingworth, *English Housing Trends*, Bell, 1965; A. I. Harris, *Labour Mobility in Great Britain 1953–63*, Government Social Survey, 1966.

32. J. B. Cullingworth, *English Housing Trends*, Occasional Papers on Social Administration No. 13, Bell, 1965, pp. 101–103.

33. The figures are from the Hunt Report on *The Intermediate Areas*, Cmnd. 3998, HMSO, 1969.

34. N. H. Carrier and J. R. Jeffrey, *External Migration, 1815–1950*, Studies on Medical and Population Subjects No. 6, General Register Office, HMSO, 1953, p. 33.

35. Institute of Race Relations, *Facts Paper on the United Kingdom 1970–71*, I.R.R., 1970.

36. For further discussion, see Chapter 4 of Volume II.

37. *Scottish Economic Bulletin*, No. 1, Summer 1971, p. 9.

38. Strategic Plan for the South East, *Studies Volume 1: Population and Employment*, HMSO, 1971, p. 18.

39. See R. L. Welch, *Migration in Britain: Data Sources and Estimation Techniques*, University of Birmingham, Centre for Urban and Regional Studies, Occasional Paper No. 18, 1971, especially Chapter 5.

40. See particularly, *Strategic Plan for the South East: Studies*. Much of this section is based on the Volume I of the Studies: *Population and Employment*, HMSO, 1971.

41. *Strategic Plan for the South East: Report of the South East Joint Planning Team*, HMSO, 1970, pp. 17–18.

42. It should be stressed that this is a highly summarized discussion. For further details see *Report of the Strategic Planning Committee*, *1.2.72*, Greater London Council.

43. Ministry of Housing and Local Government, Statistics for Town and Country Planning, Series III—Population and Households, No. 1, *Projecting Growth Patterns in Regions*, MHLG, p. 36.

44. For a list, see pp. 290–2 of the author's *Town and Country Planning in Britain*, Allen & Unwin, 4th edition, 1972.

45. Since this chapter was prepared, the Government Actuary's report on population projects has been published: (Office of Population Censuses and Surveys, *Population Projections 1970–2010*, HMSO, 1971). This is the first of an annual series, which collates projections for England and Wales, Scotland and Northern Ireland, and also provides a comprehensive description of projection methods. A more general discussion of projections and their use (by T. H. Hollingsworth) is to be found in Chapter 6 of S. C. Orr and J. B. Cullingworth, *Regional and Urban Studies: A Social Science Approach*, Allen & Unwin, 1969.

Chapter 2

The Socio-economic Framework

SOCIO-ECONOMIC CHANGE

Changes in standards of living since the last war have been dramatic. One has only to compare a Lowry painting with a photograph of, say, the Birmingham Bull Ring to immediately be impressed by the change in style. The advent of mass car-ownership, of television, washing machines and the like, of drip-dry clothes, of supermarkets, of 'package' continental holidays; the spread of owner-occupation; the expansion of secondary and further education; the increased significance of family-centred and home-centred leisure activities; the 'do-it-yourself' revolution; these and many other features of contemporary life underline the changes which have taken place over the last generation or so. The popularity of television 'flashbacks' ('Scrapbooks' and 'Do You Remember' programmes) and, more recently, of 'Great Newspapers Reprinted' reflect not so much an increased interest in history but the tempo and scale of change.

Many of these aspects of social change are difficult to measure. Possession of cars and of consumer durables present little difficulty; the inadequacies of statistics showing patterns of family expenditure can be allowed for (spending on alcohol and tobacco is always under-represented); while figures on the distribution (and, even more, the redistribution) of wealth may be so fraught with difficulties as to be of use only for examination questions for students of statistics.[1] Yet, the real standard and quality of life defies the statistician: it remains more in the province of the novelist and the 'non-quantifying' sociologist.[2] Nevertheless, the fact of a changed character of social life is abundantly obvious: so obvious indeed that the relative poverty and deprivation which exists is likely to be ignored until it is forced upon the collective consciousness by 'shocks' such as the (generally) staid reports of Committees of Inquiry or the 'revelations' of social commentators or pressure groups such as *Shelter* or the *Child Poverty Action Group*. Here, debate is carried on at two levels: a popular level, epitomized by *Cathy Come Home* or *Edna: the Inebriate Woman*; and a more intellectual level, exemplified by Fabian Essays.[3]

Some of the implications of contemporary 'social trends' are outlined in Peter Willmott's paper, published in Volume III of the present series. Others are discussed in later chapters of this and the following volume.

Of increasing concern recently has been that part of the standard of living which has been labelled 'the quality of the environment'. The spate of books in this field is eloquent testimony to this concern.[4] One curious result has been the growth of a school of thought apparently dedicated to retarding economic growth. Yet it is not economic growth itself which is at fault, but rather 'economic growth defined exclusively in terms of private consumption or of the production of material goods'.[5] Attempts to approach the problem by way of highly sophisticated cost-benefit analyses have served to show that, as with other matters which are of equal importance, the essential issues are political.

Economic development implies major changes in economic structure and mobility of resources, in land use and in social organization. Developments in land use planning and in the social services are a reflection of the political and social response to economic change. Technological development requires an educated labour force. Rapid change in the demands for particular skills and in the development of existing techniques implies a rate of 'skill obsolescence' which requires a type of educational organization and provision very different from that which was adequate when a skill learnt in adolescence could last a worker's life-time. High rates of change involve a degree of social insecurity which demands new types of social support for which traditional techniques of insurance are inappropriate.

At the same time policies designed to prevent waste and inefficiency in the use of limited natural resources and to optimize the economic and social benefits of change create their own specific problems. Land controls for instance tend to increase the price of land and, therefore, the cost of housing, thus widening the gap between rent paying capacity and 'economic' rents. Market orientated policies in public services shift demand to substitute services which involve a lower direct price to the individual user (e.g. from public transport to private transport) and inflict particular hardship on those who are unable to transfer to the substitute (e.g. those too poor or otherwise unable to afford or use private cars), and possibly even greater hardship in areas where market criteria dictate an abandonment of public services (e.g. in remote rural areas).

Since social policies develop in response to political demands, some problems attract major political attention (e.g. housing, transport, unemployment) while others receive much less attention (e.g.

mental health, nursery schools, welfare services) until the public conscience is shocked by 'revelations'.

It is now almost conventional to argue that an 'affluent society' should be able to divert resources from 'economic growth' to 'social amelioration', and the preservation of amenity. Yet (without subscribing to the view that everything can be priced and evaluated in a cost–benefit analysis), this is to take a very narrow approach to growth and development. Even on a strictly economic approach, unemployment, for example, indicates an underutilized resource which, if not reduced to the minimum, involves a waste. The problems of pollution and loss of amenity are, to a large extent, created by a particular legal and economic system which transfers the costs from those responsible to those affected. A major technological breakthrough may bring great benefits to consumers by way of cheaper goods, but it may also result in unemployment, and create social havoc in the particular area which produces the goods which are now to be replaced. This is an economic cost which should be offset against the wider economic gain. Perhaps the simplest example lies in the field of industrial injury and illness where clear cases of the true cost of production can be seen. Similarly, 400,000 road accident casualties a year are one of the costs of the growth in motor transport.

Economics is becoming increasingly sophisticated in measuring wider costs (and benefits), but many aspects of welfare defy the analytical tools of this science. Causal relationships are frequently far from evident, still less measurable. In what economic balance sheet can the homeless or the slum dwellers be put? Is the 'value' of a pleasant environment measurable in the same way as cabbages? Many aspects of the quality of life, of social justice and of aesthetics cannot be entered on any balance sheet.

To this theme we shall need to constantly return, and an attempt at synthesis is made in the final chapter of the second volume. The present chapter is intended to outline and highlight some of the major dimensions of economic and social change. Of necessity, statistics can be provided only of measurable things: these are not necessarily the most important.

EMPLOYMENT

The importance of employment requires no detailed elaboration. Labour is a major resource: the size, skills and geographic distribution of the labour force are major factors in national and regional economic development. Growth in the population of working age involves an increase in the availability of labour and an increased need for jobs.

Changes in the demand for and the supply of labour have national, regional and local implications. Unemployment is a waste of resources involving social as well as economic costs. It turns economically active people into dependants. Even with income-maintenance policies (social security) it reduces both the standard of living of those affected and the national product. It is a major factor in migration. Persistently high unemployment in particular areas leads to an outflow of workers to areas of labour shortage and better opportunities. This is not necessarily undesirable: indeed, it may be socially and economically beneficial. Certainly there is no presumption that a given pattern of population distribution should be fossilized. Nevertheless, both growth and decline have multiplier effects which cumulatively may be undesirable, and the process of change itself may involve intolerable social costs.

The Labour Force

The population of working age is conventionally defined as that part of the population which is over school-leaving age (15, shortly to rise to 16) and under retirement age (60 for women; 65 for men). In 1941, this age group numbered 32·4 million (U.K.): it grew slowly to 1968 (33·6 million) and the 1969-based projection to 1981 (35·1 million) represents a 5 per cent increase.[6] The increase in this age group is thus (at around 0·6 per cent a year) less than that of total population growth (around 0·8 per cent). But many factors affect the relationship between the population of working age and the working (or economically active) population. A very important one is the number of jobs available: the greater the demand for labour, the larger is the number of married women and people of retirement ages who are drawn into the labour force. (Somewhat confusingly, the concept of the working population includes the registered unemployed: this needs to be borne in mind in interpreting the published figures.) The working population of the U.K. was lower in 1970 (25,637,000) than in 1965 (26,049,000) and fluctuated by over a half of a million during these years.[7] The number of unemployed (included in the count of the working population) fluctuated in the opposite direction though by smaller amounts (rather more than quarter of a million).

Another relevant factor is the number of children above the statutory minimum school-leaving age of 15 who stay on at school. This is much less directly influenced by the state of the economy. The number of 15-year-olds at school increased from 282,000 in 1961 to 526,100 in 1970, representing 38·8 and 69 per cent of the age group in the respective years.[8]

The raising of the statutory minimum school-leaving age to 16 in 1972/73 (assuming that this 'prediction' is fulfilled) will, of course, further reduce the working population—and also the population of working age. The growth of further education similarly reduces the working population, though not the population of working age. (The number of U.K. born students at British Universities increased from 154,000 in 1965–66 to 203,000 in 1969/70; students in initial teacher training courses increased from 28,790 in 1959 to 91,437 in 1969.) [9]

As a proportion of the population of working age, females form well over a half, but their share of the economically active population has increased dramatically. Between 1951 and 1966, the number of working women in Britain increased by 1·9 million, while working men increased by only 345,000.

The majority of women now stay on at work after marriage and the evidence strongly suggests that it is the birth of the first child which has now become the most usual occasion on which a woman gives up work, whether or not she resumes later.[10]

There is another important aspect to this. The proportion of women who are married has increased (and is expected to increase still further in the future—from about 57 to 65 per cent by 1981).[11] As a result, married women are forming an increasing proportion of

Table 12   *Economic Activity, Great Britain, 1951–1966* [14]

	Thousands		
	1951	1961	1966
Males and females			
Total home population			
aged 15 and over	37,908	39,569	40,041
Economically active	22,610	24,014	24,857
Part-time workers (included above)	(831)	(2,066)	(3,121)
Males			
Total home population			
aged 15 and over	17,862	18,811	19,030
Economically active	15,649	16,232	15,994
Part-time workers (included above)	(47)	(174)	(373)
Females			
Total home population			
aged 15 and over	20,045	20,758	21,011
Economically active	6,961	7,782	8,863
Part-time workers (included above)	(784)	(1,892)	(2,748)

the labour force: 5 per cent in 1931, 12 per cent in 1951 and 20 per cent in 1966. Since many married women take part-time employment, this is becoming an increasingly important element in the overall employment situation. Whereas in 1951 there were only 831,000 part-time workers in Britain, by 1966 the number had increased to 3,121,000 (of whom 2,748,000 were women). This has significant implications for distribution of industry policy, local labour markets, hours of work, journey to work and (since over half a million working women have dependent children of pre-school age)[12] for nursery provision.

The size of the working population is also affected by the number of people of retirement age who stay at work. The proportion of men retiring at age 65 has increased markedly in recent years: from 57 per cent in 1964 to 70 per cent in 1968. The Government Actuary is assuming that by the late seventies this proportion will reach 93 per cent.[13]

CHANGES IN OCCUPATIONAL STRUCTURE

Major changes are taking place in the occupational structure of Britain. The picture is confused by the nature of the available statistics, but the problems to which these give rise need not concern us here (though they explain the apparently wayward selection of dates for particular comparisons).

Most striking has been the increase in the service sector and particularly in office employment. This is a field in which differing definitions abound, but, on one definition, the number of office workers increased by 1,163,000 or 41 per cent between 1951 and 1961 (compared with 8 per cent for all workers). The trend continued at a slower rate between 1961 and 1966 with an increase of 564,000, or 14 per cent.[15] Employment in services increased by three quarters of a million (7 per cent) between 1961 and 1966 and at the later date constituted a half of all employment. On current trends it will increase to over 60 per cent by the last decade of the century.[16]

The increase in professional, technical, administrative and clerical employment is no recent phenomenon. This can be illustrated by reference to social service manpower. In 1931, employment in the educational, medical and welfare services totalled 769,000. This increased to 1·2 million in 1951 and 2 million in 1966.[17]

More generally, 'administration' is growing at a very fast rate in both the private and public sectors. The number of non-industrial staff in the civil service, for instance, increased from under 400,000 in 1961 to nearly half a million in 1971.[18]

58

Similarly, in the ten years 1959–69, the insurance, banking and finance 'industry' and the professional and scientific services 'industry' expanded their employment by 37 per cent, from 2·5 millions to 3·4 millions—a rate of growth exceeding that of any other industry. It is this growth which explains the relatively low rate of unemployment in South East England where (in 1968) some two-thirds of employees worked in this sector.

By contrast, declines in the fortunes of the coal-mining, ship-building and cotton textiles industries have resulted in significant decreases in the number of people employed in the related occupations. Thus, a decline of a quarter in the annual production of coal between 1960 and 1971 (accompanied by an increase in output per manshift of a third) has resulted in a major reduction in the number of colliery wage-earners (from 517,000 in 1963–64 to 287,200 in 1970–71).[19]

Such changes can have a very significant impact on certain areas. For instance, the number of colliery wage earners in Durham and Northumberland fell by 55,000 (over a half) between 1963/64 and 1970/71—a rate of around 8,000 a year.

An attempt to summarize recent changes (made by Professor Hicks) is given in Table 13. This shows the number of workers in the several broad industrial groups in the years 1957 and 1968. Clearly, by far the biggest change has taken place in what Professor Hicks categorizes as 'other services, including professions'. Nevertheless, the primacy of manufacturing remains (though a more detailed

Table 13 *Estimated Industrial Distribution of Working Population, Great Britain, 1957 and 1968* [21]

	Millions		Percentages	
	1957	1968	1957	1968
Agriculture	1·0	0·8	4·1	3·2
Mining	0·9	0·5	3·7	2·0
Manufacturing	8·8	8·7	36·4	34·5
Building and contracting	1·5	1·6	6·2	6·3
Gas, water and electricity	0·4	0·4	1·7	1·6
Transport (incl. post office)	1·7	1·6	7·0	6·3
Administration (national and local)	1·3	1·4	5·4	5·6
Armed forces	0·7	0·4	2·9	1·6
Distributive trades	3·0	3·3	12·4	13·1
Other services (incl. professions)	4·7	6·0	19·4	23·8
Unemployed	0·3	0·5	1·2	2·0
Total	24·2	25·2	100·0	100·0

analysis than is appropriate here would show major changes in the components of 'manufacturing').

The emphasis in the current discussion is on the scale and character of change. Other authors have stressed the relative stability (as does Peter Willmott in the third volume of this series).[20] Much depends on the implications which are being highlighted. Here the important implications are for regional and local economies, for regional, industrial location and employment policies, for social security and for retraining. Changes which have a small impact on national statistics may be of crucial importance for particular localities and for particular households.

THE DIRECTION OF FUTURE CHANGE

The crucial question, however, is the extent to which recent changes can be used as a basis for predicting the direction of future change. It is generally accepted that the rate of change will increase. In support of this the time lag between scientific discovery and its application is frequently quoted: 112 years for photography (1727–1839), 56 years for the telephone (1820–1876), 35 years for radio (1867–1902), 15 years for radar (1925–1940), 12 years for television (1922–1934), 5 years for the transistor (1948–1953) and 3 years for the integrated circuit (1958–61) [22]; while current discoveries in such fields as electronics and plastics may be applied within a year.[23]

But to believe that we are going faster does not help in determining where we are going faster to. The rapid growth of office employment might be brought to a halt or even reversed by developments in telecommunications and data-processing. On the other hand, there is more than a suggestion that such aids to efficiency feed on themselves and create 'needs' which previously did not exist or at least could not be met. As a result, 'displaced' office workers could find more—not less—jobs open to them. Moreover, though highly sophisticated machines may reduce the needs for, say, face-to-face contacts, 'human factors' may intrude to reinforce the traditional resistance to change, thus preventing or delaying the advent of the fully electronic office. Indeed, it might even become an important status symbol for leading institutions to have 'old fashioned' office aids such as secretaries and typewriters.

All this is, of course, conjecture—as must be any forecasts of the future. There are at present no indications that the growth of office employment will abate, or that the decline of employment in 'primary' industries (agriculture, mining, etc.) will not continue. In manufacturing industry, there is a clear trend towards greater 'capital intensity': thus new processes and new plants will require less labour. The demand for 'services' seems likely to grow, particularly in the 'public sector' where the potential for, e.g., social service development is enormous; but here the constraint is a political one.

There are important implications for both intra-regional and inter-regional policy from these changes. Technological change in office processes have facilitated the movement of routine processes to suburban locations. Major office-type institutions can move to more distant locations (as with certain parts of the Post Office to Durham and Glasgow), thus providing new jobs in areas of industrial decline. But, at the same time, increased productivity and capital intensity in modern manufacturing industry may mean reduced pressures for firms to move from areas of labour shortage to areas of unemployment; and those that do will provide fewer new jobs than in the past. On the other hand, the apparent increase in the desire for more modern and spacious premises may become a more significant factor in industrial mobility than in the past.

It is possible to present arguments and counter-arguments for these and many other possibilities. What does seem to be clear, however, is that the scale of change has resulted in an increase (which seems likely to continue) in insecurity for workers, the danger of poverty for them and their dependants, and a more recalcitrant problem of 'depressed' areas. Skilled workers may find their skills become rapidly obsolete. This has been recognized in the professions (where security of tenure provides a very strong protection against 'redundancy'): hence the growth of 'refresher' courses and the development of 'mid-career' training programmes. The skilled worker, however, has to acquire a new skill. The implied need for a major development of training programmes is only just beginning to be appreciated.[24] For the present, attention is still focused on policies to reduce unemployment by incentives to industrialists to move to areas where it is high.

UNEMPLOYMENT

'The Government accept as one of their primary aims and responsibilities the maintenance of a high and stable level of employment after the war.' So stated the 1944 White Paper on *Employment Policy*: thus signifying a revolution in policy. The extent of this revolution is all the more striking when it is remembered that unemployment in the inter-war years averaged about 12 per cent, rising to as much as 22 per cent. This traumatic experience shattered the traditional economic theory that the free operation of market forces tended to result in 'full' employment apart from temporary fluctuations due to the trade cycle. Henceforth, a major government role in 'managing the economy' was accepted and all governments have been committed to a policy of full employment.

Until recently, unemployment has averaged between 1·3 and 2·6 per cent. (In the late sixties it passed 3 per cent and in late 1971 approached 5 per cent.) Indeed, governments have been faced more with problems of labour shortage and inflation than unemployment. Nevertheless, national averages mask wide variations between different areas. In January 1972, when the Great Britain average was 4·3 per cent, the regional rate ranged from 2·4 in the South East to 7·1 in Scotland (and 8·9 in Northern Ireland). The average for the development areas was 7·0, while much higher rates were experienced in particular areas: the highest local rates in this month were (in England) 10·5 in Hartlepool, (in Wales) 10·0 in Bargoed, and (in Scotland) 11·2 in the Highlands and Islands.[25]

Paradoxically, the national problem of inflation has made it more difficult to deal with regional problems of unemployment. Or at least, it has become clear that the two problems have to be dealt with differently. Policy measures at the national level to maintain full employment in all regions can result in extreme inflation. On the other hand, national policies to combat inflation can result in high unemployment in particular areas. The essence of the problem is that the regional economies differ and, thus, *national* policies are inadequate. A national policy which succeeds in reducing inflationary pressures in the South East can lead to intolerable levels of unemployment in the development areas. Economic policies, therefore, need to be regionally selective—by way of fiscal measures, differential taxes and subsidies, programmes of public sector investment and a battery of incentives to private investment and economic growth in disadvantaged regions.

It is common to think of regional figures in terms of variations from the national average. Indeed, a recent book bears the title *Regional Variations in Britain.*[26] In many ways this can be useful, but it is important to remember that national figures represent a mere manipulation of local figures. For some purposes national figures are positively misleading. Thus, it is not very helpful to know that in December 1970 there were, in Great Britain, 620,000 registered unemployed and 211,000 unfilled vacancies,[27] without at the same time knowing where the unemployed and the vacancies were. Furthermore, regional figures commonly relate to very artificially defined areas and can be as 'unreal' as national averages. Finally, a regional analysis of any one factor has to be supplemented by similar

62

analyses of other relevant factors. For example, in calculating 'labour reserves', account must be taken of variations in the age structure and in the proportion of young people continuing in education beyond the statutory minimum school-leaving age. Less tangibly, some regional variations may be related to deep-seated differences in tradition and attitude: the national average is a norm only in a statistical sense; it is not an ideal to which all regions should be expected to aspire.

Nevertheless, the regional elements which go to make up the national average highlight differences which, at the least, pose questions for further inquiry. Thus, in the words of *The National Plan*,[28] the differences between activity rates in the different regions give some indication of the scope for drawing extra people into the working population if employment opportunities were more equally distributed. In Table 14, the first column lists the 1961 regional activity rates; the second column gives figures which take into account regional variations in the proportion who can be regarded as potentially economically inactive (the retired, students, etc.); the third

Table 14   *Regional Activity Rates, Great Britain 1961 and National Plan Estimates of Labour Reserves* [29]

	Activity rate[a]	Active persons plus specified inactive[b]	'Labour reserves'[c]
	%	%	*Thousands*
South East England	61·0	70·2	—
South Western	55·8	66·3	85
Midland	64·6	71·9	—
North Midland	61·4	69·5	—
East & West Ridings	61·5	70·0	—
North Western	62·9	72·0	—
Northern	57·8	66·1	83
Scotland	59·9	68·1	54
Wales	55·2	64·7	97
Great Britain	60·7	69·5	319

Notes:
(a) The *activity rate* is the number of employed people (including employers, self-employed, H.M. Forces and unemployed) as a percentage of the population aged 15 years and over.
(b) The *specified inactive* includes students, retired people and those in institutions.
(c) The number of additional people who would have been in the working population if the activity rates in the second column were raised to the national average.

column provides an estimate of the size of 'labour reserves'—the number of people who would have been in the working population had activity rates risen (in the below-average regions) to the national average. The total for 1961 was 319,000. If to this were added the 'excess' of unemployed in each region over the national average, the total labour reserve in the below-average regions would have been around 420,000. Much more impressive figures could be achieved, of course, by basing the calculation, not on the national average, but on the employment and activity rates achieved in the 'highest' region.

The important unanswered (and, indeed, unasked) question is the extent to which there is 'responsiveness' or, to use the economic term, *elasticity* of labour supply to increases in job opportunity.[30] There can be no doubt that there is a degree of responsiveness 'but how far this relationship is borne out over time within a given area is a question which does not appear to have been investigated and it is this which really matters for policy purposes'.[31]

Some idea of the range of regional differences is given in Table 15. The overall activity rate for males in Great Britain (employees as percentage of home population aged 15 and over) in 1969 was 73·5, but there was a regional range from 62·0 in the South West to 77·0 in the South East. For females, the national average was 40·2, with a range from 30·1 for Wales to 42·7 for the West Midlands. The pattern for different age groups, however, was in some ways

Table 15   *Regional Activity Rates by Age and Sex, 1969* [33]

	Great Britain	Highest region	Lowest region
Males aged:			
15–24	72·4	76·9 (Y. & H.)	62·4 (S.W.)
25–44	84·6	88·8 (S.E.)	71·9 (E.A.)
45–64	85·5	88·7 (S.E.)	74·2 (S.W.)
65 and over	17·4	21·4 (S.E.)	10·3 (W.)
All Ages	73·5	77·0 (S.E.)	62·0 (S.W.)
Females aged:			
15–24	63·3	68·0 (S.E.)	51·3 (W.)
25–44	45·1	49·2 (N.W.)	35·6 (W.)
45–59	50·6	55·5 (N.W.)	35·8 (W.)
60 and over	10·3	11·9 (S.E.)	6·2 (W.)
All ages	40·2	42·7 (W.M.)	30·1 (W.)

Abbreviations

E.A.	East Anglia	W.	Wales
S.E.	South East	W.M.	West Midlands
S.W.	South West	Y. & H.	Yorkshire and Humberside
N.W.	North West		

THE SOCIO-ECONOMIC FRAMEWORK

significantly different. Only Wales emerges clearly as a region with low activity rates for females of all ages. As might be expected, the South East is prominent as the region with the highest activity rates for the majority of sex–age groups, but it is surpassed by Yorkshire and Humberside for males aged 15–24 and by the North West for females aged 25–44 and 45–59.

Such variations reflect a complex of inter-related factors: industrial structure, relative decline and growth in different industries, the state of local labour markets and, in relation to women, tradition.[32]

The rise in unemployment to around the million mark at the end of 1971 brought about not only a political response to increase employment but also an academic reaction on the measurement of unemployment.[34] This has for long been a matter for serious discussion (though regrettably little action). The essence of the problem is that the published statistics are a by-product of an administrative process designed not to measure 'unemployment' but for the administration of unemployment benefits and the job-placing services of employment exchanges. Each month a count is taken of the number on the registers of the exchanges who are actually unemployed and 'capable of and available for work'.

At first sight this appears a sensible (and cheap) way of collecting unemployment statistics, but it has serious drawbacks which many other countries (including those of the Common Market) overcome by periodic household and labour force surveys. Many married women who are not eligible for unemployment benefit (only industrial injuries insurance is compulsory) do not bother to register when the demand for their services falls. The addition of other groups (such as part-timers) might increase the total number of 'unemployed', on Peston's argument, by as much as 60 per cent.[35]

Others have argued that the present system greatly inflates the 'true' number since it includes the unemployable, those 'voluntarily' unemployed (more popularly termed the 'spongers' who prefer to live on social benefits), and those who are fraudulently claiming benefit (i.e. registered as being unemployed, but working). Wood has put the number of these (at December 1971) at around 250,000. By further subtracting those who had been out of work for less than eight weeks (the 're-deploying' as distinct from the 'unemployed') Wood manages to reduce the December 1971 figure of 'unemployment' from 923,000 to less than 250,000.[36]

Thus, while on one interpretation unemployment at this date might have been 60 per cent above the official figure, on an alternative interpretation it could have been 75 per cent lower. This vast difference is

65

more than a matter of differing approaches (though, in this particular case, this is of some importance): it stems in part from the inadequacy of unemployment statistics.

Nevertheless, even adequate statistics could leave plenty of room for argument on how far unemployment could be reduced by changes, for example, in the social security system, in minimum wage legislation and in labour mobility. Wood argues (as many other economists have done) that 'the labour market is not working properly if labour fails to move into areas, industries and occupations where most needed. Such lack of mobility—partly due to lack of houses to rent, partly to unwillingness to change place of residence—may well be more important as a *cause* of unemployment than inadequate demand.'[37] This is a nice illustration of the inter-connectedness of a multiplicity of issues. Some of the more important of these are encompassed by regional planning policies to which we now turn.

REGIONAL PLANNING[38]

In economic terms the full utilization of regional resources adds to national wealth. In social terms, areas of decline and restricted opportunities are intolerable. Even if neither of these contentions is accepted, political forces would compel governments to act with positive discrimination towards relatively 'unfavoured' areas.

Economic aspects are not easy to assess except in the crudest of terms; social aspects are a matter of attitudes towards inequality and of sympathy born of understanding, and are thus dependent upon knowledge and its dissemination; political aspects are the most volatile of all. It follows that inter-regional policies (to a very much larger extent than intra-regional policies) are subject to the vagaries of the economic, social and political climate. Furthermore, the objectives of regional policy are never simple (except in electoral terms): indeed they may be—and frequently are—contradictory. Glasgow, for instance, is a City with both a large unemployment problem and a huge problem of congested inadequate housing. The same is true of the North West Region of England—exacerbated by acute land pressures. Should the policy objective be to facilitate the outward migration of population or the growth of employment? Is it possible to effectively pursue both policies at once?

How should areas in need of positive discrimination be determined? If unemployment is to be the major criterion, what is to be taken as the crucial level? And is 'hidden unemployment' to be taken into consideration? Whatever level is judged to be the appropriate one, are areas below this to be denied all help or are they to be classified as 'intermediate' areas eligible for partial assistance? Is aid to be continued when unemployment falls to tolerable levels, thus releasing resources for other areas? If so, is there not a danger that future uncertainties in respect of financial assistance will act as a deterrent to industrialists?[39] Are areas of unemployment *ipso facto* to be aided, or should aid be concentrated on particular growth points?

These and a host of similar questions illustrate the problem facing the policy makers. The problem is considerably exacerbated by the uncertain efficacy of policy and the difficulty of assessing the impact of any particular measure. In no field is policy less sure-footed.

Furthermore, all policies involve costs. Some are directly measurable (such as grants to industrialists), but some are not: a firm persuaded to move to a poor location may suffer a permanent economic handicap. How is this to be judged against the benefits which the advent of the firm has brought to the locality?

All the evidence suggests that the amount of potentially mobile industry is severely limited. The limit is, however, affected by the general state of the economy but, in the short-run at least, this might be stimulated by permitting development in the areas of growth rather than in those of decline. Indeed, in the long-run, national economic growth might be severely constrained by 'too much' industry being channelled into development areas. There is little evidence to prove or disprove such contentions but, in any case, the issue is not solely one of economics. 'Once we move away from the economist's frame of reference, other factors bearing on social welfare loom large.'[40]

Curiously, however, though much of the debate on the development areas is couched in terms of 'aid', there has been surprisingly little discussion of the costs of the more prosperous areas. A succinct case for this was put by Professor A. J. Brown in his 'Note of Dissent' to the Hunt Committee's report on *The Intermediate Areas*:

Within the prosperous areas that have been the main sources of mobile industry, the community's interest in seeing industry persuaded to move or expand away from its present site is far from uniform. Where there are identifiable social costs of congestion (traffic congestion and shortages of living space), as well as labour shortage, the case for encouraging outward moves is much greater than where there is no physical congestion, only fairly high pressure of demand for labour. Physical planning has so far been left to cope with this distinction; there seems to be a case for enlisting the help of the price-mechanism.[41]

67

Apart from the intrinsic justification for a 'congestion tax' (that costs should be borne by those who create them unless there is a strong contrary argument in any particular case), it would provide a useful supplement to the administrative control operated through the industrial development certificates scheme.

Much of the aid given to the development areas (and all of any congestion tax) is of the nature of transfer payments. Some lose while others benefit, but the consumption of real resources is limited to the administrative resources involved. Positive discrimination in terms of investment in infrastructure, clearance of derelict land and the like is very different: this employs resources which have an alternative use elsewhere. Given limited resources (which always is the case) one road more in Central Scotland is one less in, say, South East England. (Anyone who drives in the two areas can readily see the effects of differential investment in favour of Central Scotland.)

This poses a much more difficult set of questions for government. Does such use of real resources have a greater or less impact on regional development than aid given by way of transfer payments? Professor Brown thinks that the evidence is 'in favour of financial inducements, assisted by administrative action, as the most important element in any economical system for influencing industrial location, provided that the distribution of infrastructure investment, in accordance with the normal criteria, takes account of those changes in location of industry and population that it is desired to bring about'.[42]

Even if he is wrong, however, and infrastructure investment does have a major 'pulling power', which types of investment are the most efficacious? Would the resources invested in building the Forth, Tay and Erskine Bridges have been better deployed in, say, the redevelopment of Glasgow?

These must, at least in the present state of knowledge, be rhetorical questions. In any case, the most important factors may be more psychological than economic. Certainly the images created by magnificent engineering projects are striking even if industrialists say that they attach more importance to 'labour reserves'. That attitudes are not unimportant is evidenced by the apparent willingness of American industrialists to locate in Scotland while English industrialists tend to regard it as remote. Furthermore, as regional statistical sources increase, the images of the 'unfortunate North' and the 'fortunate South' are seen to be, at the least, overdrawn and not infrequently false. It is here that we see the inadequacies of the traditional types of measurement. Without denying the relevance of the things which can be measured, many of the important elements which go to make the quality of life are not measurable. Nevertheless, serious and intolerable inequalities exist between regions and it is the broad aim of regional policy to reduce these.

High unemployment in some areas is frequently accompanied by labour shortages in other areas. Which is the better policy: to promote the mobility of capital (thus increasing the rate of investment and the growth of jobs in the areas of high unemployment and reducing the pressures in the areas of labour shortage); or to promote the mobility of labour (thus relieving unemployment by the removal of workers to areas where their labour is needed)?

In a predominantly urban economy there are problems in either policy. Areas of labour shortage are typically areas of housing shortage and 'congestion'. Political considerations also make it difficult to explicitly assist decline and encourage the movement of workers to 'pressure areas'. Politicians in both areas would need a lot of convincing that it is good policy to actively promote 'the drift to the south'. A convincing case is not easy to establish, even if 'congestion' is disproved and a positive policy is followed of accommodating urban development in the areas of strong economic growth. The issue is much more than one of 'politics'.

The argument against encouraging migration is commonly stated in terms of 'social capital'. The areas of decline have a large social investment in houses, roads, schools and public services: outward migration, so the argument runs, would result in an under-utilization of this capital and need to 'replace' it elsewhere. Though the argument has not received the study it deserves, it does not appear to be a very strong one in the British context of population growth, relatively small annual migrations, and few areas of actual decline. Furthermore, the areas of outward migration are typically in need of replacement of their social capital. To the extent that these contentions are true, it matters little whether the additional or replacement social capital is provided in the areas of decline or those of growth.

Nevertheless, an accelerated rate of decline might make the social capital argument a stronger one. Probably more important is the economic and social impact of continuous emigration on an area. As Barkin has put it:

Distressed economic areas tend to become less and less capable of self-assertion and initiative as their condition is prolonged. It is for this reason that early assistance in redevelopment is essential. The lowered capacity for economic growth is due not only to the spirit of resignation which ultimately suffuses a community that continually fails, but also to the out-migration of the young and

69

ambitious, leaving behind the older and less mobile persons. As the distress continues, the graduates of the school system move out, making for a more unbalanced population. Community income drops and the quality and quantity of public services deteriorate so that the services and inducement necessary for attracting modern industry become fewer in number.[43]

Migration is thus not a simple 'equilibrating force', adjusting the size of the labour force and population to the levels of economic activity in both the exporting and importing areas. By strengthening the growing areas and further weakening the declining areas it compounds both success and failure: 'the rich become richer and the poor become poorer'.[44]

Such an effect could be realized on much more than a local scale. For instance, if the net outward movement of population from Scotland which was experienced in 1963–64 and 1964–65 (over 40,000 a year) had continued to 1980 the impact would have been dramatic. Though the high rate of natural increase would have maintained the total population at a level of around 5·2 million, the population of working age would have fallen from 61 per cent to 55 per cent of the total: there would have been 274,000 fewer people of working age, 118,000 more old people and 156,000 more children.[45]

It was in this context that the Scottish 1966 White Paper reiterated the Government's regional policy: 'Measures to divert industrial expansion from the congested areas of the Midlands and the South East of England will continue to be applied rigorously.'[46]

Yet, if applied too rigorously, is there not a danger that the sources of economic growth will be seriously diminished? The case for large-scale asistance to development areas looks clear enough when their problems are viewed in isolation. It looks very different to the 'congested areas' as the following extract from a West Midlands report makes clear:

... the ability of the country to cope with the problems of imbalance depends on the maintenance of the economic strength of the regions such as the West Midlands, which must be a net contributor to the resources which have to be provided for the purpose. The maintenance of the economic strength of the West Midlands is, therefore, essential if the country is to be able to deal with the economic weakness of less favoured regions. . . . A positive climate is required if the most is to be made of the Region's economic potential. So long as the Government's attitude appears negative, industry, local authorities and statutory bodies will all feel inhibited from undertaking the developments which are necessary for an expanding regional economy. . . . Steering to the assisted areas, by controls, the growth which results from the pressures for modernisation may help to relieve the pressures on resources, particularly manpower, at times when there is strain on them in the West Midlands, but what is its cost? Whilst the balance cannot only be struck in economic terms, it must no longer be struck without evaluating the economic consequences.[47]

Unfortunately, however eloquent this may be as a posing of the question, it does not answer it and, given the current state of regional economics, no clear-cut answers are possible. Regional policy arguments are now couched much more in economic terms than was previously the case, but 'regional economics is not yet a coherent body of analysis applicable to the affairs of a country'.[48] For the foreseeable future, policy will remain what it has been to date: pragmatic, over-responsive to changes in the regional and national economic situation and, above all, political. However, as economists increasingly turn their attention to the application of their skills to spatial questions (at both the intra-regional and inter-regional levels) the debate should become better informed. At the least it is hoped that a better understanding will be achieved of the cost and efficacy of development area policies. Increased knowledge will not, of course, settle the argument, but it should permit a more profitable debate.

THE EVOLUTION OF REGIONAL POLICIES IN BRITAIN

Three types of regional policies can be discerned in Britain and abroad, which might conveniently (though not very accurately) be labelled 'social', 'economic' and 'urban growth' policies. Each shades imperceptibly into the next and, in practice, each contains elements of the others. Further, reflecting the essentially political nature of regional policies, there has been no clear 'development' from one type to another: while one government has tended to emphasize one type of policy, a successor has tended to emphasize a different type. The categorization is, nevertheless, useful in identifying the diverse political philosophies of regional development.

A *social* approach regards policy in terms of assistance to declining areas and is aimed at mitigating undesirable social consequences. A very explicit statement of this approach was made in 1959 by the then President of the Board of Trade:

> We should start from the assumption that the economic and industrial expansion of the country should proceed freely in response to growing and changing consumer demand, and that it should proceed on the principle of the most effective use of our national resources. . . . This principle of the most efficient use of our resources must clearly be mitigated in some cases by Government action to deal with certain social consequences which the nation does not regard as acceptable.[49]

On this view, regional aid is a social service which cannot be justified in economic terms.

By contrast, the Barlow Report [50] of 1940 (in many ways ahead of its time) emphasized the relationship between regional decline, migration and metropolitan growth. The problems of the depressed areas and of the excessive growth of, and congestion in, London and other major urban areas were seen, not as separate problems but as different aspects of the same problem of population distribution. The Barlow Report represents the first indication of the *urban growth* approach to regional development, but its major importance lay in the emphasis it gave to the economic justification for regional policies. Nevertheless, its impact on policy was limited and many of the policies which are popularly associated with it were, in fact, implemented in a very different framework from that envisaged by the Commission. Thus, the new towns programme was conceived essentially in terms of physical planning policy rather than as an element of regional policy. Indeed, though new legislation, controls and administrative processes, which were introduced in the early post-war years, bear an apparently strong relationship to the Barlow recommendations, in truth there was only a superficial resemblance. To the Governments of the post-war years up to the mid-fifties, there seemed little need for regional policies: the traditional industries (heavily concentrated in the development areas) boomed and, though above the national average, unemployment remained low. Regional policy was, to a large extent, in abeyance.[51]

A number of economic factors combined to highlight the basic insecurity of the outlying regions in the mid-fifties and, as a result, regional policies were accorded a higher priority. As the earlier quotation shows, however, the policy was essentially a social one, closely tied to relieving unemployment. However, in the early sixties a clear *economic* approach to regional problems began to appear. A good illustration of this is to be found in a 1963 report of the National Economic Development Council:

> The level of employment in the different regions of the country varies widely, and high unemployment in the less prosperous regions is usually thought of as a social problem. Policies aim, therefore, to prevent unemployment rising to politically intolerable levels and expenditure to this end is often considered a necessary burden to the nation, unrelated to any economic gain that might accrue from it. But the relatively low activity rates in these regions also indicate considerable labour reserves. To draw these reserves into employment would make a substantial contribution to nattional employment and national growth.[52]

The N.E.D.C. estimated that an increase in national employment of 200,000 (0·9 per cent) was not impossible.[53] This would mean that the rise in national output per head required to achieve the target growth rate of 4 per cent a year would be significantly reduced.

Running alongside this renewed attention to the economic justification of regional development was the re-emergence of interest in the co-ordination of economic and physical planning. At this time, thinking was restricted to such issues as transport planning, the clearance of derelict land and other policies designed to improve the environment and the 'infrastructure', and the development of new towns and other 'growth areas'.[54] This type of thinking characterized the first two official essays in comprehensive regional planning: the 1963 White Papers for Central Scotland and North East England.[55]

This philosophy of regional restructuring rapidly became the major feature of all the regional studies which appeared in increasing numbers in the late sixties. The task of elaborating urban growth policies within regions has clearly been recognized. Much more tentative is the move towards the development of a national urban growth policy. This involves difficult issues of inter-regional economic (and political) relationships. In a recent comparative study of strategies for urban growth in a number of countries, Rodwin concluded, in relation to Britain, that:

> There is still no policy on the urban growth pattern of the nation as a whole; no effort to relate the growth of London, Birmingham, Liverpool, Manchester and other urban regions into an overall complex; no evaluation of the desirability of influencing one way or another the physical form or direction of development in these urban regions. To take on such responsibilities will not be an easy

73

task. But it will be surprising if these questions do not soon rank among the most challenging policy problems on urban growth to confront the British nation.[56]

Best's suggestion that the whole of England and Wales is of a similar character to the North East American Megalopolis [57] underlines the relevance of this 'urban growth' policy to national and inter-regional planning. Recent downward revisions of population projections, together with an apparent reduction in the 'drift to the south', may delay development along these lines. But the growth of regional strategies and the anticipated re-organization of local government inevitably involve central government in decisions on inter-regional policy. To date, these have been ad hoc. A number of Regional Economic Planning Councils have been disappointed at the rejection of some of their proposals by central government. They have, however, had no alternative but to acquiesce: they have no political power to do otherwise, but given a new structure of local and regional government, the position could change radically. If regional decisions are to be taken other than on the basis of expediency, an inter-regional policy will be necessary. If one is not explicitly developed, it will emerge by default.

URBAN POLICIES

Ebenezer Howard proposed a population size of 30,000–32,000 for his garden cities.[58] The Reith Committee on New Towns thought that 30,000 to 50,000 was the optimum.[59] Colin Clark, in an attempt to establish the size of city needed to provide its region with a full range of service activity, concluded that the appropriate city size was between 100,000 and 200,000, but that a higher figure of between 200,000 and 500,000 was needed to allow the full development of manufacturing activity.[60] Further up the scale, Le Corbusier proposed a city of 3 million people,[61] while the Goodman Brothers advocated 5 million as being the right size for a modern technological settlement.[62] Neutze, much more tentatively, concluded, on the basis of Australian data, that the balance between the advantages to manufacturing industry and the costs of local government and traffic congestion lay in the 200,000 to 1,000,000 range.[63] Lomax, focusing on the cost of local services, thought that 100,000 to 200,000 was the optimum size.[64] The Royal Commission on Local Government in England came to the conclusion that, in terms of local government services, there was no best size, but that the area of an authority responsible for education, housing and the personal services should normally contain at least 250,000 people.[65] Klaasen demonstrated theoretically that there was an optimum size for an 'agglomeration' but the data needed to apply his model are exceedingly difficult to estimate.[66] Illustrations of the various approaches can be multiplied,[67] but the greater are the number of factors which are taken into account, the more complex—indeed, impossible—does the analysis become. The classic study of Duncan[68] demonstrated the way in which optima varied according to the criteria used. There is no way 'in which these various optima may be objectively equilibrated, compromised, weighted or balanced to yield an unequivocal figure for *the* optimum population for a city'.

In any case, the issue which arises in practice is not that of the optimum size of cities in general but the optimum size of cities in particular; and this issue can be decided (though translation into practice is another matter) only in the context of broader economic, social, aesthetic and physical issues, the national, regional and sub-regional distribution of population and economic activity, and a host of other factors.

The concept of the optimum is thus both elusive and theoretical.[69] This, however, is not the only problem: another arises in determining the reality to which it might relate. Where, for example, are the 'boundaries' of London or Manchester or Liverpool or Glasgow to be drawn? The Registrar-General's 'conurbations' are statistical abstracts relating to 'built-up contiguous areas', and, as Senior has succinctly put it, 'nothing is so irrelevant to the structure of the urban region as continuous built-upness'.[70] The 'urban region' concept might at first sight appear to offer a more helpful approach, but how is this to be defined? Are Manchester and Liverpool centres of two urban regions separated by Warrington? Or are all three part of a North Cheshire–South Lancashire urban region?

To pursue such questions is profitless except in relation to some specific issue such as the organization of transport services, water supplies, health services or local government boundaries. Even here the answers are by no means always self-evident. Nevertheless, non-overlapping areas have to be determined (at least for the individual services if not for all of them in combination) in order to facilitate effective planning.

This does not help in deciding an optimum population size, but it does help in providing the framework within which rational decisions can be taken in respect of the distribution of population. Indeed, this is the relevant issue. In practical terms this is largely a matter of accommodating the growth of the major urban areas (whether within or beyond their regions).

75

This is very much what regional physical planning in Britain has been about (though with intermittent concern for high rates of regional unemployment and, for a period, the beginnings of the development of regional economic policy).

An important element in the underlying planning philosophy has been a concern with the physical size of urban areas. Though there has been little in the way of an elaboration—or even a discussion—of the optimum size of any particular urban area (still less of urban areas in general) there has been a belief that many urban areas are 'too big'. This stems in part from the Barlow Report and a preoccupation with the problems of London. But there are many other strands—green belts (*for* towns as well as *against* them), agricultural land conservation, the protection of 'amenity' and so forth. Together these have become so interwoven as to strangle thought about alternatives. And the cynics have not failed to notice that planning orthodoxy has nicely harmonized with the interests of county governments surrounding urban areas. The traditional town–country battle has become sanctified by planning wisdom.

Thus Birmingham is said to be 'congested': decongestion can be effected by rehousing 'overspill' beyond the green belt in new and expanding towns where the decanted population can secure both homes and jobs in a pleasant environment. The argument is couched in a mixture of terms—economic, physical, aesthetic, social and emotional. It is based on the premise that firms can move from 'congested' inner areas to new and expanding towns with benefit to the firms themselves, their workers, the 'exporting area' and the newly developing areas. It also assumes that the scale and timing of the possible movement of jobs is commensurate with that of the housing development which has to take place in response to population growth and redevelopment. It further posits that the multiple organs of government can, in fact, cope with the problems of coordination which a policy of this nature involves. In short, the policy is desirable and workable. Unfortunately, it is by no means self-evident that the policy is desirable and experience to date suggests that it is unworkable.

In what sense is Birmingham 'congested'? There is no shortage of readily-available factory space and industrial sites. Industrialists who are refused permission to erect new factories can commonly find alternative premises within the Conurbation.[71] Movement to overspill areas involves large costs, both short-term (e.g. the cost of movement and 'settling-in') and long-term (e.g. reduced labour markets and severance of linkages with the industrial complex of the Conurbation).

There are definite economic advantages in concentration (which, as the Barlow Commission pointed out, is not the same thing as congestion or overcrowding).[72] The real problem is that of the wider social and economic costs which are not borne directly by those who create them. Decisions on location are taken in the light of 'private' costs and benefits (non-economic—i.e. immeasurable—as well as economic): these necessarily exclude the costs of urban 'infrastructure' and of subsidizing passenger transport or high flats for lower-income families in central areas. Nevertheless, it could be argued that, on balance, it is preferable for these costs to be accepted by the community since the economic advantages of concentration are so great.

These are intangibles, and too little research has been undertaken to provide unambiguous guides to policy. Any issue which is selected for examination—traffic congestion for example—can be dealt with by a variety of means other than a policy of restraining urban growth. Indeed, the term 'congestion' may be a misnomer for inefficient urban structures: it may well have little or nothing to do with sheer size. If this is so, the issue is not one of restraining urban growth but of restructuring urban areas.

In any case, the workability of a policy of restraining urban growth raises many doubts. If there is a restricted amount of mobile industry (as there certainly is) then this sets a limit to the number of people who can be accommodated in 'self-contained' communities. If some of this mobile industry is channelled to development areas the limit is further reduced. Since this inter-regional movement of industry has a high political and economic priority, the scope for implementing the accredited overspill policy is severely constrained. This has been increasingly recognized by central government, as a further illustration from the West Midlands shows.

The West Midlands Economic Planning Council's report *Patterns of Growth* envisaged an overspill from the West Midlands Conurbation of over half a million people between 1965 and 1981. (This was twenty times the number who moved during the period from 1945 to 1965.) To 'support' this population movement, a massive movement of employment was 'needed'. That the Council had some impression of the difficulties is suggested by their phraseology: 'this massive outward movement of population from the conurbation will need to be supported by movement of industry on a scale equally unprecedented in the region'. Whatever may be the shortcomings of planning reports, timidity is not one of them. How 'unprecedented' the movement of industry would need to be can be appreciated by analysing previous movement: between 1945 and 1965 about

77

80,000 jobs left the Conurbation of which 50,000 went to development areas.

This planning by oracle was rejected by the central government, though in language which was judged appropriate to the conventions of diplomacy:

The Government have been unable wholly to accept the overspill proposals . . . we have grave doubts about the viability of an overspill programme of the order of magnitude envisaged by the Council within the context of our policy for the distribution of industry. . . . Many more people will almost certainly have to be accommodated within commuting distance from their work in the conurbation and further study of urban development along these lines is required.[73]

The 'further study' was provided by the West Midlands Planning Authorities' Conference and resulted in a report entitled *A Developing Strategy for the West Midlands* (1971). This has a relatively greater degree of realism, but it is highly indecisive: the 'strategy' proposed is 'pliant in terms of its breadth of response and the range of its dimensions'. A critic has referred to it as 'a cotton wool report' which is 'feminine in its submissiveness'.[74] The Report's indecisiveness might be defended in terms of the current vogue for flexibility. No such defence is possible, however, on the Report's treatment and rejection of peripheral growth as a possible strategy—despite the fact that 'it represented the form in which the Conurbation had grown in the past and which the existing assets of location might tend to reinforce in the future'. A major reason for the rejection of this 'option' (taking the Report on its own terms and ignoring the political framework within which the study was undertaken) is that peripheral development was assumed to involve 'the maximum amount of commuting': in other words, while people would move, their jobs would not. As a result (even with an increased reliance on public transport) massive road investments would be required to accommodate commuters' cars. Given the assumptions, the logic cannot be faulted, but if alternative assumptions were to be taken a totally different option emerges. In particular, if it were assumed that jobs would move to, and new jobs could be created in, peripheral areas the major disadvantage of peripheral development would be significantly reduced. The heavy dependence in this urban area on private cars (60 per cent of commuters in 1966 used private cars), the motorway network already completed, the growth of service sector employment, land availability, and many other factors suggest that this strategy is a strong candidate to be the 'preferred one'.[75]

78

The Report rapidly ran into the opposition of Birmingham City Council who complained of the inadequate relief that the plan would provide for the City's housing problems and—to the extent that relief was provided—of the serious damage which would be suffered if the City were 'drained' of its population and industry.

Thus the essentially political nature of the whole process is demonstrated. The interests of the City and the surrounding Counties differ as a result of the arbitrary administrative boundaries which separate them. The Counties appeal to 'planning principles' while the City is preoccupied with its housing problem and the impact of overspill on its financial viability. The central government attempts to hold the uneasy balance, but can influence the situation only to the extent that it can positively promote the industrial development of the new and expanding towns (within the context of its inter-regional priorities) and can refuse (as at Wythall in 1960)[76] or agree (as at Chelmsley Wood and in North Worcestershire) to peripheral developments by the City.

The tragedy is that since planning philosophy holds that peripheral development will not take place on the scale which it does the plans which are made are invalid. The peripheral developments are conceded at a late stage as stop-gap measures and lack the advantages of forethought which it is the function of planning to provide. Birmingham is by no means an untypical example: basically the same story can be related for all the conurbations.

Perhaps an even greater tragedy is the impact of planning policies on urban housing development. Since urban growth is a matter for restraint, the pressure of demand builds up inside the urban areas. Both political necessity and high land prices (one of the real costs of the restraint policy) force up densities. In the private sector this is limited by the willingness of people to accept high prices and high densities (and by the alternative which is open to the private sector of lower prices and lower densities beyond the green belts). In the public sector, shielded by overt and hidden subsidies, and catering for 'applicants' who have had few alternatives[77] there has been little limit to the densities which can be achieved. As a result, 'planned' environments have been created which, though far more sanitary, are in other respects reproducing the very congestion and inadequacies which it was their object to abolish.

This is, of course, an unbalanced (but unfortunately not untenable) view. It ignores the undoubted achievements in the creation of good environments in both old and new towns. Nevertheless, on the crucial test-bed of planning policy—the conurbations—there is much that has gone wrong. In particular, every conurbation has a number

79

of major 'overspill estates' which have been built in defiance of planning orthodoxy (typically at great speed following a long drawn-out city–county battle) and which suffer all the inadequacies which post-war planning was supposed to avoid.[78] This has resulted from the idea that the restraint of urban growth was both desirable and possible. The force of an idea unfortunately bears little relation to its validity.

It should now be clear that the crucial issue is not the size of urban areas but how their growth is to be accommodated and how the urban region is to be restricted. Such 'structure planning' requires political planning units of a size and extent considerably larger than the existing local authorities. (How far the local government reorganization which is under way adequately meets the situation is discussed in the final chapter of Volume II.) Essentially, this implies identifying areas where inter-dependent issues can be satisfactorily managed. For major issues such as the distribution of population and economic activity, major road networks, water supply and the like, these areas need to be very large (though—if they are to be rooted in local government—considerably smaller than the current economic planning regions). Until some such organization exists, planning for the major urban areas must lack direction: the appropriate studies will seldom be satisfactorily carried out, even where they are, the political will to bring about restructuring will be missing.

It is easy to be pessimistic about the likelihood of the necessary organizational changes, but there are increasing signs that new thinking on ordering (as distinct from preventing) urban growth is developing. The most recent (at the time of writing) is also the clearest:

> While official encouragement has been given to planned dispersal from London and other conurbations to new towns and town development schemes created for the purpose, a great deal of unsponsored movement out of cities to their surrounding areas has also taken place. Such movement has not been accompanied to the same extent by a parallel movement of industry and although some migrants find work locally, many commute back to work in the main conurbations. . . . Thus there has gradually emerged a new settlement pattern consisting of groups of towns standing in a hierarchical relationship to one or more major urban centres, the whole exhibiting a complex system of economic and social links. . . . The nature of these areas demands that they should be planned as a whole.
>
> In the shorter term up to about 1981, when taking account of new developments already planned and the likely limited supply

of mobile industry, it seems inevitable that a considerable part of the housing need will have to continue to be met by further commuter developments within access of the main employment centres. The various economic and social interactions within city regions make it desirable to ensure that the consequences and implications of the broad patterns of new development within the spheres of influence of the main conurbations are considered in the context of the needs and resources of the areas as a whole. Comprehensive plans for each conurbation and its surrounding area will, therefore, be needed to determine the desirable and efficient pattern of development.

The quotation comes from the inter-departmental study (*sic*) on *Long Term Population Distribution in Great Britain*,[79] published in order to 'stimulate informed discussion' and to 'contribute to forward thinking on planning integrated at national, regional and local levels'. Advances in thinking, however, make only a minor impact without appropriate changes in the instruments of government which are responsible for implementation.

IN CONCLUSION

A wide range of issues has been covered in this chapter. Many have been touched upon only superficially. Others (such as leisure and recreation, the increasing separation of home and work, and the implications of the educational advances—and failures—of the postwar period) have been omitted. Some emerge in later discussions, while many cannot be encompassed within the scope of a rapid and necessarily selective review. Several of the more important questions—with emphasis on the *distributivion* of resources, costs and benefits—are developed in Volume II, while the readings in Volume III complement and expand the discussion. In the following chapter, we turn our attention to the physical framework within which social and economic forces operate.

References and Further Reading

1. See R. M. Titmuss, *Income Redistribution and Social Change*, Allen & Unwin, 1962. Anyone intending to use official figures is advised to read this beforehand.

2. Those who are interested in following this line of thought are referred to A. V. Cicourel and W. J. Filstead (eds), *Qualitative Methodology*, Markham Publishing Co., 1970.

3. See *Labour and Inequality*, Fabian Society, 1972. For an analysis which starts from a very different political position see A. Christopher *et al.*, *Policy for Poverty*, Institute of Economic Affairs, 1970.

4. There is now a vast—and growing—library. The following represent merely a selection from the wide range of writings:

T. Aldhous, *Battle for the Environment*, Fontana, 1972.

J. Barr, *The Environmental Handbook: Action Guide for the U.K.*, Pan Books, 1971.

J. Bugler, *Polluting Britain*, Penguin Books, 1972.

B. Commoner, *The Closing Circle: Confronting the Environmental Crisis*, Jonathan Cape, 1972.

P. R. and A. H. Ehrlich, *Population, Resources, Environment: Issues in Human Ecology*, Freeman, second edition, 1972.

J. W. Forrester, *World Dynamics*, Wright-Allen, 1971.

E. Goldsmith, *Can Britain Survive?*, Tom Stacey, 1971.

J. Maddox, *The Domesday Syndrome*, Macmillan, 1972.

D. H. Meadows et al., *The Limits to Growth*, Earth Island, 1972.

M. Nicolson, *The Environmental Revolution*, Hodder & Stoughton, 1970.

N. Pole, *Environmental Solutions*, Eco-Publications, 1972.

H. F. Wallis, *The New Battle of Britain*, Charles Knight, 1972.

W. B. Yapp, *Production, Pollution, Protection*, Wykeham Publications, 1972.

DOE, *Sinews for Survival: A Report on the Management of Natural Resources*, HMSO, 1972.

DOE, *50 Million Volunteers: A Report on the Role of Voluntary Organisations and Youth in the Environment*, HMSO 1972.

DOE, *How Do You Want To Live? A Report on the Human Habitat*, HMSO, 1972.

DOE, *Pollution: Nuisance or Nemesis? A Report on the Control of Pollution*, HMSO, 1972.

5. *Science, Growth and Society*, OECD, 1971, p. 19. Two authors who take very different stands on this issue are E. J. Mishan and W. Beckerman.

See E. J. Mishan, *The Costs of Economic Growth*, Staples Press, 1967 (and the 'more popular' version, *Growth: The Price We Pay*, Staples Press, 1969); and W. Beckerman, 'Why We Need Economic Growth', *Lloyds Bank Review*, October 1971.

For a most illuminating series of case studies in environmental protection, see R. Gregory, *The Price of Amenity*, Macmillan, 1971.

6. First Report from the Select Committee on Science and Technology, Session 1970–71, *Population of the United Kingdom*, H.C. 379, May 1971, pp. 11 and xiv.

7. *Annual Abstract of Statistics, 1971*, Table 140.

8. Ibid., Table 117.

9. Ibid., Tables 130 and 123.

10. A. Hunt, *A Survey of Women's Employment*, Government Social Survey, HMSO, 1968, p. 13.

11. Memorandum by the Department of Employment and Productivity to the Select Committee on Science and Technology, First Report, Session 1970–71: *Population of the United Kingdom*, HC. 379, HMSO, 1971, p. 71.

12. The figure (515,000) relates to England and Wales in 1966: see *Social Trends*, No. 1, 1970, Table 25. (A further two million had children of school age.)

13. *Report by the Government Actuary on the Financial Provisions of the National Superannuation and Social Insurance Bill 1969*, Cmnd. 4223, HMSO, 1969, Appendix, paragraphs 20–21.

14. *Social Trends*, No. 1, 1970, Table 23.

15. The figures are taken from Vol. 1 of the Studies undertaken in connection with the Strategic Plan for the South-East, *Population and Employment*, HMSO, 1971, p. 109. See also Ministry of Labour, *Occupational Changes 1951–1961*, Manpower Studies No. 6, HMSO, 1967.

16. Select Committee, op. cit., p. 71.

17. S. Rosenbaum, 'Social Services Manpower', *Social Trends*, No. 2, 1971, p. 6.

18. *Annual Abstract of Statistics, 1971*, Table 147.

19. *Annual Abstract of Statistics, 1971*, Tables 167–169.

20. P. Wilmott, 'Some Social Trends', Chapter 5 of *Planning for Change* (Volume III of the present work).

21. J. R. Hicks, *The Social Framework*, Clarendon Press, 4th edition, 1971, p. 74.

22. J. J. Servan-Schreiber, *The American Challenge*, Penguin Books, 1969, p. 59.

23. See D. Lewis, 'New Urban Structures' in K. Baier and N. Rescher, *Values and the Future*, Free Press, 1969, p. 315.

24. See S. Mukherjee, *Changing Manpower Needs*, PEP Broadsheet 523, 1970; the same author's *Making Labour Markets Work*, PEP Broadsheet 532, 1972; and Department of Employment, *Training for the Future*, HMSO, 1972.

25. *Department of Employment Gazette*, February 1972, pp. 177–181.

26. B. E. Coates and E. M. Rawstron, *Regional Variations in Britain*, Batsford, 1971.

27. Figures from *Annual Abstract of Statistics, 1971*, Tables 151 and 153.

28. *The National Plan*, Cmnd. 2764, HMSO, 1965, p. 37.

29. Ibid., p. 38.

30. See L. C. Hunter, 'Planning and the Labour Market', in S. C. Orr and J. B. Cullingworth, *Regional and Urban Studies: A Social Science Approach*, Allen & Unwin, 1969, pp. 66–70.

31. Ibid., p. 70.

32. 'Regions which have traditionally been those where women have not gone out to work, particularly after marriage, were (in 1965) still those where the proportion of women at work was lowest.' A. Hunt, *A Survey of Women's Employment*, Government Social Survey, HMSO, 1968, Vol. I, p. 9.

33. *Abstract of Regional Statistics, 1970*, Table 21.

34. See, for example, M. Peston, 'Unemployment: Why We Need a New Measurement', *Lloyds Bank Review*, No. 104, April 1972, and J. B. Wood, *How Much Unemployment?*, Institute of Economic Affairs, 1972.

35. M. Peston, *op. cit.*, p. 3.

36. J. B. Wood, op. cit., p. 61.

37. Ibid., p. 45.

38. For further discussion see G. McCrone, *Regional Policy in Britain*, Allen & Unwin, 1969.

39. Merseyside was 'listed' in 1960, 'stop-listed' in 1961 and 'replaced on the active list' for aid in 1963. On this point see *Seventh Report from the Estimates Committee 1962–63: Administration of the Local Employment Act, 1960*, H.C. 229, HMSO, 1963.

40. E. J. Mishan, *Growth: The Price We Pay*, Staples Press, 1969, p. 164.

41. *The Intermediate Areas*, Cmnd. 3998, HMSO, 1969, p. 162.

42. Ibid., p. 157.

43. S. Barkin, 'Principles for Area Redevelopment Legislation', *Labor Law Journal*, Vol. 10, No. 8, August 1968, p. 528.

44. W. R. Thompson, 'Internal and External Factors in the Development of Urban Economies', in H. S. Perloff and L. Wingo, *Issues in Urban Economics*, Johns Hopkins, 1968, p. 59.

45. Scottish Office, *The Scottish Economy 1965 to 1970: A Plan for Expansion*, Cmnd. 2864, HMSO, 1966, p. 1.

46. Ibid., p. x.

47. West Midlands Economic Planning Council, *The West Midlands: An Economic Appraisal*, HMSO, 1971, pp. 4 and 7.

48. A. J. Brown, 'Surveys of Applied Economics: Regional Economics, with Special Reference to the United Kingdom', *Economic Journal*, Vol. LXXIX, December 1969, p. 789.

49. Reginald Maudling, on the opening of the Second Reading Debate on the Local Employment Bill, *H.C. Debates*, Vol. 613, Col. 32, 9th November, 1959.

50. *Report of the Royal Commission on the Distribution of the Industrial Population*, Cmd. 6153, HMSO, 1940.

51. See G. McCrone, *Regional Policy in Britain*, Allen & Unwin, 1969, Chapter IV, and A. J. Odber, 'Regional Policy in Britain', in *Area Redevelopment Policies in Britain and the Countries of the Common Market*, U.S. Department of Commerce and Area Redevelopment Administration, 1965.

52. National Economic Development Council, *Conditions Favourable to Faster Growth*, HMSO, 1963, p. 14. See also *The National Plan*, Cmnd. 2764, HMSO, 1965, pp. 84–100; and the Toothill Report: *Report of the Committee of Inquiry into the Scottish Economy*, Scottish Council (Development and Industry), 1961.

53. The calculation took into account, for each of the 'less prosperous' regions, the activity rates in three population age groups: men aged 15 to 64 years, women aged 15 to 34 years and women aged 35 to 64 years. For men, and for women aged 15 to 34, it was assumed that post-war maximum activity rates attained before 1961 could be reached again by 1966. Women aged 35 to 64 increasingly entered employment from 1953 to 1961; it was assumed, therefore, that where reasonable, this upward trend in activity rates would continue until 1966. Unemployment rates in 1961 were assumed to fall by a third.

54 See N.E.D.C., op. cit., p. 26.

55. *Central Scotland: A Programme for Development and Growth*, Cmnd. 2188, HMSO, 1963; and *The North East: A Programme for Regional Development and Growth*, Cmnd. 2206, HMSO, 1963.

56. Lloyd Rodwin, *Nations and Cities: A Comparison of Strategies for Urban Growth*, Houghton Mifflin, 1970, p. 155.

57. R. Best, 'Regional Conversions of Agricultural Land to Urban Use in England and Wales, 1945–67', Institute of British Geographers, *Transactions and Papers*, 1970, p. 27. See below, pp. 90–91.

58. E. Howard, *Garden Cities of Tomorrow*, Faber (1965 reprint).

59. Ministry of Town and Country Planning, *Final Report of the New Towns Committee*, Cmnd. 6876, HMSO, 1946, pp. 8–9.

60. C. Clark, 'Economic Functions of a City in Relation to Its Size', *Econometrica*, Vol. 13, 1945, pp. 97–113. See also W. R. Thompson, *A Preface to Urban Economics*, Johns Hopkins, 1965.

61. Le Corbusier, *The City of Tomorrow*, Architectural Press, 3rd edition, 1971.

62. P. and P. Goodman, *Communitas: Means of Livelihood and Ways of Life*, Random House, 1960.

63. G. M. Neutze, *Economic Policy and the Size of Cities*, Australian National University Press, 1965.

THE SOCIO-ECONOMIC FRAMEWORK

64. K. S. Lomax, 'The Relationship between Expenditure per Head and Size of Population of County Boroughs in England and Wales', *Journal of the Royal Statistical Society*, Part 1, Vol. 166, 1943, pp. 51–59.

65. Royal Commission on Local Government in England 1966–1969, *Volume 1: Report*, Cmnd. 4040, p. 69.

66. L. H. Klassen, 'Regional Policy in Benelux Countries'. *Area Redevelopment Policies in the Countries of the Common Market*, Department of Commerce, U.S. Government Printing Office, 1965.

67. For example, J. Kozlowski and J. T. Hughes, 'Urban Threshold Theory and Analysis', *Journal of the Town Planning Institute*, Vol. 53, 1967, pp. 55–60 and 'Threshold Analysis—An Economic Tool for Town and Regional Planning', *Urban Studies*, Vol. 5, 1968, pp. 132–143; P. A. Stone, *Housing, Town Development, Land and Costs*, Estates Gazette, 1963; Ministry of Transport, *Traffic in Towns* (Buchanan Report), HMSO, 1963; Association of Municipal Corporations, *The Costs of Urban Concentration and the Financing of the Equipment of Large Towns and Urban Areas*, Council of Europe, 1968; H. W. Richardson, *Urban Economics*, Penguin Books, 1971, pp. 86–95; Royal Commission on Local Government in England, *Volume III: Research Appendices*, Cmnd. 4040–II, HMSO, 1969, Appendix 7, 'Representation and Community: An Appraisal of Three Surveys'; etc.

68. O. D. Duncan, 'Optimum Size of Cities', in P. K. Hatt and A. J. Reiss (eds), *Cities and Society*, Free Press, revised edition, 1957, pp. 759–772.

69. For a more rigorous discussion see *Urban Studies*, Vol. 9, No. 1, February 1972 which contains a number of papers which deal (devastatingly) with the concept of an optimum city size. See also W. Alonso, *The Economics of Urban Size*, Centre for Planning and Development Research, University of California, Berkeley, Working Paper 138, November 1970.

70. D. Senior (ed.), *The Regional City: An 'Anglo-American Discussion of Metropolitan Planning*, Longmans, 1966, p. 19.

71. On this point and more generally see B. M. D. Smith, 'Industrial Overspill in Theory and Practice' *Urban Studies*, Vol. 7, 1970, pp. 189–204. One nice illustration of the problem of co-ordinating planning policies given in this article is that of several nationalized industries selling off surplus land in canal and rail sidings and surface mining works in order to improve their trading position.

72. 'Mere size of city—leaving aside strategic considerations—need not . . . be objectionable if the city is well planned. . . . Size of town is no guide to the pressure of congestion: a medium sized town may suffer from the evil as well as a million mark town' (*Barlow Report*, p. 156).

73. Unpublished document.

74. *Official Architecture and Planning*, October 1971, p. 741.

75. Curiously, a later section of the Report proposes five major peripheral industrial sites 'as part of the economic restructuring of the Conurbation', but this is not related to the thinking on 'options'. (*A Developing Strategy for the West Midlands*, paragraph 265.)

76. See J. R. Long, *The Wythall Inquiry: A Planning Test Case*, Estates Gazette, 1961.

77. For further discussion see Chapter 2 of Volume II of the present work.

78. For further discussion see Chapter 5 of Volume II of the present work.

79. DOE, *Long Term Population Distribution in Great Britain—A Study*, HMSO, 1971. The summary chapter of this is reproduced in Volume III of the present work. See also pp. 121–124 below.

Chapter 3
The Physical Framework

Few countries are as densely populated as the U.K. Ignoring statistical freaks such as Monaco (where 23,000 people live on half a square mile) and a few island states, only three European countries have a higher density of population—West Germany, Belgium and the Netherlands. Densities within the United Kingdom vary, of course: from 171 to the square mile in Scotland to 916 in England. Indeed, England's density is exceeded (in Europe) only by the Netherlands. In relative terms England is thus truly a crowded country. The national physical framework of planning is very different from that of the U.S.A. with 57 people per square mile or Australia with four.

For some issues, however, it is not the national—or regional—figures which are relevant. It is of little relevance to the land problem in the London area that there are vast areas of open land in the north of Scotland. Thirty per cent of the population of England and Wales live in the conurbations on a mere 3 per cent of the total land area. In this connection, the problems of the major urban areas in this country are very similar to those in Europe and even the U.S.A. With the issues of housing, access to recreational land, and the like, it is not the national land area which is important so much as the land within the region.

Documenting land uses and changes is, unfortunately, a hazardous business. The only comprehensive data are those obtained in the extraordinary Land Use Survey directed by Dudley Stamp.[1] These relate to the 1930s and are therefore much out-of-date. A second national Land Use Survey is currently under way,[2] but this is, like its predecessor, a lengthy undertaking. No statistical results are yet available. In the absence of a national cadastral survey, the main source of data has to be the annual agricultural statistics. These (in the plaintive words of the Ministry of Agriculture) have to bear a weight for which they were not designed. Fortunately, heroic efforts of interpretation have been performed by a number of academics, foremost among whom are R. H. Best and J. T. Coppock.[3] It is on

86

their work that this section heavily leans. It should be stressed, however, that the figures, particularly those relating to urban land, are approximate estimates. Figures for individual regions are even more approximate.

Table 16   *Density of Population in Various Countries*

	Population per sq. mile
United Kingdom	591
England	916
Wales	340
Scotland	171
N. Ireland	278
Australia	4
U.S.A.	57
France	237
West Germany	638
Belgium	819
Netherlands	956

Table 17   *Major Land Uses, England and Wales, 1900–1950*[4]

(*Thousand acres*)

Year	Agriculture	Woodland	Urban development	Unaccounted for*
1900	31,050	1,900	2,000	2,180
1925	30,780	1,880	2,300	2,170
1939	30,180	2,290	3,200	1,460
1950	29,920	2,370	3,600	1,240
1960	29,440	2,540	4,000	1,150

		Percentage		
1900	83·6	5·1	5·4	5·9
1925	82·9	5·1	6·2	5·8
1939	81·3	6·2	8·6	3·9
1950	80·6	6·4	9·7	3·3
1960	79·3	6·8	10·8	3·1

* Includes ungrazed deer forest and other totally unutilized rural land.

In 1900, some 2 million of the 37 million acres of England and Wales were in urban use. By 1960 the urban area had doubled, and at that date formed 10·8 per cent of the total land area. Since 1960, the proportion has increased to around 12 per cent. (The addition of the figures for Scotland, with its vast area of rural land, reduces the proportion of urban land to around 8 per cent of the total.)

Currently, some 40,000 acres of agricultural land are taken for urban development each year. This, however, has to be seen in perspective. Expressed differently, 'urbanization' is taking place at a decennial rate of about one per cent. Furthermore, the rate is less than two-thirds of that experienced in the 1930s when over 60,000 acres were absorbed by the large scale suburban growth of the time (made possible by developments in transport and the availability of cheap land in a period when agriculture was depressed and planning controls were minimal). More significantly, as Best has pointed out, there has been no sustained increase in the loss of farmland to urban use. Contrary to popular belief, there has been a tendency for a slight falling off. This is a reflection, not of reduced pressure, but of effective planning controls and the not entirely unrelated rising price of land.

Nevertheless, urban growth is still proceeding at a faster rate than population growth. This can be clearly seen if the total urban area is expressed as a ratio to population. In 1950, there were 8·2 urban acres per 10,000 total population. By 1960, this had increased to 8·8 and by 1971 to 9·1. On current indications the urban area of England and Wales might increase by a third by the end of the century: it would then comprise 16 per cent of the total land area, compared with nearly 11 per cent in 1960.

All these figures relate to England and Wales as a whole. There are, however, very considerable differences between different regions. Unfortunately, the available statistics are most inadequate and it is possible only to indicate the range of these differences.

Table 18   *Urban Area in Relation to Population, England and Wales, 1900–1971*

	Urban area (*million acres*)	Total population (*million*)	Urban area in relation to total population (*acres per 10,000 population*)
1900	2·0	32·5	6·2
1939	3·2	41·5	7·7
1950	3·6	43·7	8·2
1960	4·0	45·7	8·8
1971	4·4*	48·6	9·1

* Author's estimate.

Except for Scotland (which is discussed separately) there are no regional figures of urban areas,* but the total area of each region expressed in terms of acres per person range from 0·29 in the densely

*But see the Appendix to this Chapter.

Table 19 *Annual Net Loss of Agricultural Land in England and Wales, 1921 to 1966* [5] (*Thousand Acres*)

5 Year Period*	Change in recorded acreage of agricultural land	Agricultural land lost to:			Corrections and reclassifications
		Urban, industrial and recreational development	Government departments	Forestry Commission and private woodlands	
1923–26	−43·2	−22·5	0	− 1·4	−19·2
1927–31	−43·9	−52·2	− 0·1	− 6·7	+15·1
1932–36	−61·5	−62·0	− 3·4	− 3·9	+ 7·8
1937–41	−47·1	−38·2	−60·0	−21·0	+72·1
1942–46	−76·3	−25·6	−65·6	−13·4	+28·4
1947–51	−13·4	−39·5	+29·4	−21·1	+17·8
1952–56	−52·1	−40·8	+ 4·8	−22·9	+ 6·7
1957–61	−58·4	−35·1	+ 3·4	−20·1	− 6·7
1962–66	−47·4	−37·9	+ 2·5	−14·1	+ 2·1

* The figures are five year averages, e.g. for 1922/23 to 1925/26.

populated North West to 1·89 in Wales (and 3·72 in Scotland). These figures are, of course, considerably affected by the position of the regional boundaries. Thus, the South East Region has 0·40 acres per person, but the old standard region of London and South East (which was much more tightly drawn) has only 0·24 acres per person. Nevertheless, the regional figures underline the range of variation over very broad areas.

These regions are not only very different in their population densities: they also differ in their rates of 'urbanization'. It is commonly assumed that this is particularly high in the South East, the Midlands and the North West. Indeed, there have been suggestions that a huge belt of urban development is emerging along an axis from Lancashire to Kent. This has been variously termed the coffin, the axial belt, the hour glass or the dumb-bell, the last two terms referring to the greater width of the development in Lancashire and the South East. More recently, the term 'megalopolis' (first coined by Patrick Geddes) and applied by Gottman to the north eastern seaboard of the United States has recrossed the Atlantic to become the fashionable term to describe this central belt of England—sometimes extended across the Channel and the North Sea to embrace northwest Europe.

Appealing terminology, even when tentatively proposed as a first indication of the direction of trends can easily become accepted as a fact: in this case abetted by major transport improvements (the M1 and M6 motorways and the electrified railway to Euston) and the arguments over Britain's entry to the Common Market. Claims are made and the terms accepted in a manner very foreign to the careful academic papers in which they originated. Those acquainted with the academic world will know that scholars dearly love to disprove each other, and on occasion themselves. This is part of the pendulum movement which characterizes the advancement of knowledge. Any new formulation of a problem, a trend or a theory immediately raises questions which stimulate thought along different lines. At the same time, since social scientists are so frequently enslaved by the data with which they have to work, new data can open up avenues which throw new light on old issues, sometimes transforming our understanding of them. This is particularly true with subjects so barren of adequate or even relevant statistics as urbanization.

Dr Best's recent study of regional conversions of agricultural land to urban use is a nice case in point.[6] Most of the studies which have contributed to the axial growth thesis have been devoted to changes in population, employment, and new major developments.[7] The absence of statistical data has made it impossible to assess the land implications of these. New data from the Ministry of Agriculture, however, have enabled a regional analysis to be made of post-war transfers of agricultural land to other uses. Though this is inadequate to show the total effect (since there is no comprehensive data on the situation before the transfers took place) it clearly reveals trends.

The conclusions of Best's study are not entirely as might have been expected. The data 'indicate that the existence of a broad belt of fairly substantial urban growth and agricultural displacement, co-inciding with the so-called "coffin" or "hour-glass" stretching diag-onally across England, is of somewhat doubtful validity at the present time'. It is more accurate to distinguish areas of rapid growth in and around London: in the counties connecting the Manchester, Mersey-side and Birmingham Conurbations (the area of most marked growth); in the more easterly counties stretching from the West Riding to Leicestershire; in County Durham; and in and around the South Wales urban region. The remaining parts of England and Wales show low rates of urban growth.

Broadly, two major divisions can be identified, separated by 'a rather narrow band of only weakly urbanizing country'. The two major divisions are the 'Central Urban Region' and the London Region.[8]

Even more striking was the finding that the most prominent area of urban growth has shifted, over the post-war period, from the London Region to the Central Urban Region, and particularly to the north-western counties. There is clearly no simple correlation between population changes and urban growth patterns. Indeed, the experience of Lancashire and Durham is in the opposite direction—absolute decreases in population accompanied by very high agricultural-urban transfer rates. Best concludes that the explanation lies in the 'increasing adoption of more adequate and reasonable standards of urban living space which have already been more widely achieved in the south'.

In a final section of his analysis, Best analyses the relevance of the concept of 'megalopis' to the alleged axial belt. Though there superficially appears to be a resemblance with the north-eastern seaboard of the United States, closer examination has a surprising outcome. Though it is true that there is an increasing tendency for the rural gap between the London and the Central Urban Regions to be closed (a tendency which the new and expanded towns such as Milton Keynes, Northampton and Daventry will reinforce), there is a vast difference between the scale of the north eastern seaboard and England's 'dumb-bell'. Furthermore, any comparison with the American megalopolis must have regard to the extent of urban influence. (By definition, a megalopolis is an area where urban influences dominate.) On both grounds, Best suggests that the only comparable area is the *whole* of England and Wales. Table 20 demonstrates the forcefulness of the case on the first ground.

Table 20   *Land and Population in Megalopolis,*
North Eastern U.S.A., and in England
and Wales [9]

	N.E. Seaboard U.S.A.	England and Wales
Total area (Km²)	138,700	151,700
Population (million)	37	46
Density (persons/Km²)	270	300
Land use:	(%)	(%)
agriculture	33	79
forest and woodland	52	7
urban and other uses	15	14

The second ground is supported by a MHLG map which suggests that only the most peripheral parts of England and Wales are at all 'distant from the urban influence'.[10]

The practical—and crucially important—implication of this is that planning in Britain has to be on a national scale. If this is not achieved the result will be inefficiency and conflict in the use of land. These conflicts are already apparent and are repeatedly raised throughout this book. A review of the major issues is given in the following sections. First, however, some Scottish figures can be given: these illustrate, in a dramatic way, the validity of Best's thesis.

Best's study relates only to England and Wales. Fortunately, Scottish separatism has led to the publication of data for this country which enable a comparison to be made.[11] Since 1900, the proportion of the total land area of Scotland in urban use has risen from 1 to 3 per cent: currently about 5,700 acres of agricultural land are transferred to urban uses each year. Population growth has played little part in this: at current density standards Scotland's very small population increase could account for only about 100 acres a year.[12] Population movements and rising standards are much more important. A striking illustration is provided by Dundee, where the population has increased by only 2 per cent since the war, while the built-up area has increased by two-thirds.[13]

Table 21   *Reduction in Agricultural Land in Scotland, 1960–1961 to 1969–1970*[14]

	Reduction 1960–61 to 1969–70 (acres)
Roads, housing, industrial development	51,352
Service departments	419
Hydro-electric and Water Boards	4,558
Coal, gravel and quarries etc.	3,125
Forestry	461,115
Sports and recreation grounds	6,611
Waste land	2,554
Miscellaneous	6,239
Total for ten-year period	535,973

Table 22   *Urban Area of Scotland 1970 and Changes 1950–1951 to 1970* [15]

	1970	Changes 1950/51–1970 No.	%
Home population	5,199,000	96,000	1·9
Urban acreage	565,000	95,000	20·2

	1950/51	1970
Percentage of area in urban use	2·4%	2·9%
Urban acreage per 1,000 population	92	109

AGRICULTURE

Agriculture dominates land use in Britain: nearly four-fifths of the land of England and Wales, and rather more in Scotland, is in agri-

92

cultural use. Though it contributes only 3 per cent to the gross national product and employs less than 3 per cent of the working population, its land use is dominant. Nevertheless, with the transfer to urban and other uses, considerable anxiety has been expressed about this 'loss'. In particular, the agricultural lobby has argued that 'the saving of farmland, as irreplaceable national capital is surely worth paying for, since it is a perennial productive asset'.[16] Since the annual loss of agricultural land is around 40,000 acres a year this, at first sight, is not an argument to be lightly dismissed. But the issue has to be seen in perspective. The standard of living which is enjoyed in Britain is largely the result of industrial specialization. As this increased, so did our 'dependence' on the importation of food. It can hardly be seriously suggested that we should resort to a subsistence economy. It is more valid to argue that we might have to import even more food than we do if our standard of living is to continue to increase. (Currently about half of our food is imported.)

Losses of agricultural land, however, have so far been more than made good by increases in productivity. Ruth Gasson, in a cautious study,[17] has suggested that increased demands for food will probably continue to be exceeded by increased physical yields of farm produce even when likely reductions in farm land are taken into account. (The demand for food is increasing at the rate of about 11 per cent each decade, while the physical yields of farm products are increasing at rates up to 15 per cent.) Recent figures for Scotland (for the period 1955 to 1970) show that a loss variously estimated at 0·17 and 0·31 per cent per year in agricultural land has been accompanied by an increase in net output of 2 per cent per year.[18]

Nevertheless, there is general agreement that in siting urban development, regard should be had for the *quality* of agricultural land. It is an unfortunate fact that the best agricultural land is frequently also the best building land. Thus, though there is no case for agriculture having an over-riding claim, it should take its place 'as one amongst many competing uses of land'.[19]

Being the predominant land use, agriculture is subject to pressures from many different sources: urban development, recreation, mineral workings, the requirements of the armed forces, roads and communications, power lines and pipelines, water supplies and so forth. These pressures carry a less obvious danger: if a restrictionist policy is adopted, the best land can eventually be lost along with the poorest. A rational allocation between competing uses (including safeguarding for agriculture) necessitates careful assessment of quality, potential and the possibilities of replacement. Land having special qualities may not be easily replaced elsewhere. An obvious

93

example, noted in the Strategic Plan for the South East, is the North Kent fruit belt between Gravesend and Canterbury.[20]

Careful planning can avoid, or at least minimize, trespass and damage by adjacent urban concentrations (e.g. by preventing irregular urban development and pockets of agricultural land—a classic example of the legitimacy of 'infilling') and by adequate provision for recreational use on low quality agricultural land (thus diverting pressures on top quality land).

FORESTRY

Though much is made of the loss of agricultural land to urban development, less attention is given to the fact that the loss to forestry is greater. Between 1959 and 1969 the total forest area of Great Britain increased from 4,075,000 acres to 4,516,000 acres.[21] Much of the total is unproductive woodland, but the area of productive forest (managed by the Forestry Commission) rose by over half a million acres—to 1,745,000 acres during this period. The annual rate of productive forest expansion is currently about 55,000 acres by the Commission and about 35,000 acres by private owners.

This increase has resulted from a deliberate policy to reduce dependence on imports: 90 per cent of British needs (by volume) are imported. The total import cost of wood and wood products (including pulp and paper) was over £650 million in 1969, of which £217 million was for timber imports.

Britain's medieval legacy of forest has been eroded by successive generations—for farming, housing, shipbuilding, and fuel. There was some replanting of oaks but, following the introduction of iron ships there was no national policy until the twentieth century. Private woodland formed some 97 per cent of the total in 1900 and it was not until 1919 (following the wartime blockade which led to the felling of some 450,000 acres of woodland) that effective steps were taken to replenish the depleted resources. The Forestry Commission was established with the dual role of creating State forests and encouraging private forestry. Following the trend well-established in the nineteenth century, the majority of the Commission's planting was of soft woods. Some 126,000 acres were planted (of which only 9,000 were hardwoods).

In their report on *Post-War Forest Policy*,[22] the Forestry Commissioners proposed a national target of 5 million acres of fully productive woodlands by the end of the century. Three million acres were proposed for plantation by the Forestry Commission on bare land. The remainder would be replanted and economically managed

94

existing woodlands which would, so far as they were privately owned, be either 'dedicated' by their owners to forestry or acquired by the State. (In the former case, financial assistance would be provided.) It was envisaged that the proposed target would eventually meet about a third of the national timber requirements. (More recent estimates, reflecting increased consumption, have halved this figure.)[23]

These proposals have formed the basis of post-war forestry policy, though the 'fifty year' programme was too long a period for acceptance by government. Currently, the Commission are working to an approved ten year programme (1964 to 1973) aimed at planting 450,000 acres.

The prime objective of forestry policy is to increase the production of wood as a raw material for industry but, as the Land Use Study Group suggested in 1966, it is 'possible that in future generations the recreation benefits of woodland may in some places be more highly valued than the wood grown in them'.[24] Concern for the amenity and recreational value of woodland has a long history though it has increased dramatically in recent years. The Forestry Act of 1927 empowered the Forestry Commissioners to make regulations governing the admission of the public to State Forests and these were applied first to the New Forest and the Forest of Dean—the only two of the many Royal Forests which have survived substantially intact from Norman times.

With its extensive open heaths and recreational facilities, New Forest is virtually a National Forest, though paradoxically it has never been so designated.[25] It was on the basis of the experience in New Forest that proposals for the establishment of National Forest Parks were made. By the beginning of the second war there were (apart from New Forest) three: Argyle (540,000 acres), Snowdonia (20,500 acres) and Dean Forest (23,000 acres). It was in the post-war period, however, that pressures mounted. The Forestry Act of 1951 empowered the Commission, for the first time, to positively provide for amenity. The 1963 statement of Government policy went further: 'The Commission, in preparing its future programmes, will bear in mind the need, wherever possible, to provide access and recreation, and will devote more attention to increasing the beauty of the landscape.'[26] The Countryside Acts of 1967 and 1968 gave the Commission specific powers to provide facilities for recreation, thus providing (in the Commission's words) 'an important landmark in progress towards the realization of the concept of the multiple use of forests in Great Britain'.[27]

In response to criticisms of unimaginative planting of conifers, with no regard to contours, considerable care is now given to fitting planting into the landscape. A leading landscape architect [28] was appointed as consultant in 1963 and the Commission now aver that 'so far from amenity and recreation being incompatible with commercial forestry, they are now permanent and integral elements in its practice'.[29]

Even allowing for some poetic licence, there is no doubt that the Forestry Commission have made strenuous efforts to reconcile the demands of forestry with those of amenity and recreation. There are now seven national forest parks which, together with New Forest, cover half a million acres. In line with recent thinking on the need to concentrate available resources in areas of greatest demand, more forest parks are under consideration—covering relatively small areas and similar to the 'country parks' being established under the Countryside Acts.

The Commission have 31 camping sites, 105 picnic places, 94 forest walks and 107 car parks. Campers totalled ¾ million in 1968 (compared with ¼ million in 1963).[30] The Commission also have a Deer Museum at Grizedale in Westmorland to which a Wild Life Centre was added in 1968. In such places, forestry, recreation and conservation overlap.[31]

It is the conflicts between these three which are of greater importance than that between forestry and agriculture. This is because, in spite of the vast—and growing—area of woodland, most of the land which has been taken out of agricultural use is of marginal quality.[32] It is also relevant to note that forestry plays a small but significant part in providing employment in areas of depopulation. This can easily be forgotten in a discussion of the 'problems' caused by forestry. As the Highlands and Islands Development Board have pointed out, 'the northern half of Scotland contains the largest reservoir of potentially plantable land in Britain and it is probable that the bulk of future new afforestation will take place in this area . . . (forestry) has a significant role to play in developing the regional economy'.[33]

WATER

An island with 600,000 acres of inland water and an average rainfall of 900 millimetres (in England and Wales—1400 in Scotland) might not be expected to have a water problem, except possibly in relation to pollution. Yet the truth is that Britain has a serious (and growing) quantitative problem quite apart from a major problem of pollution. The problem stems in large part from the fact that the majority of the population live in the areas of lowest rainfall. Furthermore, over large areas evaporation can exceed rainfall. It is, therefore, necessary to transport water from areas where it falls to areas where it is needed; and, since demand and 'supply' vary at different periods, there is also a need for storage. It is only when there is a serious drought (as in the summer of 1959, which was the driest for nearly a quarter of a century) that the problem attracts national attention—quickly forgotten when followed by a wet period (1960 was the third wettest year for a quarter of a century and resulted in widespread and prolonged flooding).

The problem is largely an organizational one: the land area used by reservoirs (both currently and in the future) is very small: a fraction of one per cent. Yet this ignores the cruel fact that the areas which have the highest rainfall and which are also most suitable for storage are also national parks or other areas of outstanding amenity. So strong has been the feeling against further reservoirs in such areas that Water Bills have been repeatedly rejected by Parliament. (Until the passing of the 1971 Water Resources Act the necessary powers could be obtained only by the Private Bills procedure, which gave ample opportunity for objection and lobbying; the 1971 Act provides for powers to be obtained by Ministerial Order.) Great emphasis has been placed by amenity bodies on desalination as an alternative, but official opinion holds that the cost is at present prohibitive (though a major research effort is continuing).

In England and Wales (in 1967) total consumption, excluding water used for cooling at power stations, exceeded 5,000 million gallons a day. Domestic users consumed 1,800 million gallons a day, while the remainder was used by industry and agriculture. Total consumption is currently rising at a rate of about 3 per cent a year, and may double by the end of the century.

The greater part of domestic use is for w.c. flushing and personal washing (22 gallons per day per person). This will rise not only because of population increase but also as a result of improved facilities: in 1966, $2\frac{1}{4}$ million households had no fixed bath, nearly 2 million had no hot water supply, and over $\frac{1}{2}$ million were without a water closet. Water consumption will rise as these deficiencies are made good; likewise with increased use of clothes washing and dish-washing machines and kitchen sink garbage grinders. Car washing also uses large amounts of water—half a gallon per day per head of population in 1967—and will similarly increase with increased car-ownership (rising by nearly a million a year).

Industry, however, is the largest user of water: 2,300 million gallons a day in 1967. Some industrial processes use prodigious

97

Table 23 *Domestic Consumption of Water, England and Wales, 1967* [34]

	Gallons per head per day
W.C. flushing and garbage grinding	11
Personal washing and bathing	11
Laundering	3
Dishwashing and cleaning	3
Gardening	1½
Drinking and cooking	1
Car washing	½
	31

amounts of water. 45,000 gallons are needed to produce one ton of steel. But the most incredible figure is that of the water used by the Central Electricity Generating Board for cooling: some 13,600 million gallons a day, of which 5,200 m.g.d. is non-saline.[35] This is not included in the total water consumption figure given above since most of the water is not, in fact, 'consumed': it is circulated through power stations and returned into river systems. The returned water, however, is at a higher temperature and can affect animal and plant life.[36] This 'open circuit system' can be operated only on estuaries and the largest rivers. Elsewhere, a 'closed circuit system' is used: in this the water is cooled by evaporation in cooling towers. This system uses a smaller quantity of water than the open circuit system but the amount lost to the atmosphere is much larger (some 40–50 million gallons a day). As a result the river flow can be significantly depleted in dry periods.

Agriculture uses relatively little water (around 300 million gallons a day) though the demand is increasing and is potentially large as a result of summer irrigation. Again the demand is (naturally) not in the areas of large supply: much of the best farmland is in areas of low rainfall. Good water management can increase potato yield by two tons an acre, while well irrigated pastures enable a large head of stock to be carried.[37] Further demands from agriculture will depend on the relationship between crop prices and water costs.

The conservation and utilization of water resources in England and Wales are the responsibility of a central Water Resources Board and twenty-nine River Authorities which operate over the areas of one or more complete river basins. Though of recent origin, a recent official report [38] has recommended a new organization which would enable better planning, co-ordination and management of water resources. The problem is a multiple one. There are technical problems in meeting the increasing demand for water, but these are capable of solution given adequate machinery for reconciling conflicting interests. These conflicts are exacerbated at present because of administrative separatism—between river authorities, sewage and sewerage disposal authorities, statutory water undertakers and other bodies such as the British Waterways Board.

Illustrative of this problem is the fact that while the Central Advisory Water Committee (the Wilson Committee) [39] was deliberating on 'the future management of water', a report on sewage disposal was issued by a separate Working Party [40] (chaired by Mrs Lena Jager). Yet, as the reports from both these inquiries underline, water supply and sewage disposal are inter-related.

Much of the water taken from rivers and underground sources is eventually returned to the rivers as effluent. Furthermore, with the increasing demand for water, there is an increasing use of treated sewage effluent for water supply. It is clear that future demands will have to be met by a much greater re-use of water and thus there must be increasing concern with the treatment given to water after use.

Two-thirds (300 million gallons a day) of London's water supply is drawn from the Thames, which also receives 180 m.g.d. of sewage effluent and 42 m.g.d. of trade effluent. Here effective treatment has enabled the maintenance of an adequate supply of pure water for human consumption. The Trent, on the other hand (which has a potential yield comparable to that of a major barrage scheme), is so heavily polluted by sewage and industrial effluent as to be unsuitable for public water supply.

This conflict (essentially between the desires for cheap disposal of sewage effluents and cheap pure water) is only one—though currently the most crucial—among many. The attraction of pure water is not matched by any attractiveness on the part of sewage disposal works. The need for industrial development in an area may conflict with the need to safeguard the flood plain of a river. A particular industry, welcome for its employment indications, may be unwelcome for its effluent. But the most obvious conflict is that which arises in the case of reservoirs.

On the one hand, reservoirs 'take land out of farming; alter the character of the landscape; influence the ecology of their surroundings in ways not yet fully understood; restrict access to many of their gathering grounds; and by concentration in hilly areas, notably in Wales, generate antagonism on the basis that they serve interests, not of the locality, but of distant users in large midland and other industrial towns'.[41]

This is not denied but, on the other hand, this is by no means all

99

there is to the issue.[42] First, even when the potential contribution of all other alternatives (estuarine barrages, desalination, increased reuse of water and greater utilization of existing sources) is taken into account, additional reservoirs are essential.[43] Secondly, loss of amenity caused by reservoirs has to be balanced against the loss which would be caused by the alternatives. A barrage would certainly have repercussions on the character and ecology of an estuary, and desalination plants would be unlikely to miss the attention of those concerned with the amenity of the coastline. Large-scale abstractions of underground water 'would diminish the flows in streams and rivers, or even cause them to dry up entirely'. 'The increased reuse of water might necessitate the construction of extensive new treatment works on the fringes of the main urban areas.'

Thirdly, reservoirs can provide amenity gains as well as losses. The Council for the Protection of Rural England argue that 'the location of many reservoirs makes them unsuitable for recreation, and those who will use even an accessible reservoir for sailing (for example) are in most cases few compared with those deprived of recreational access to the land which has been flooded'.[44] On the other hand, 'the demand for facilities for water-based sports is now growing rapidly and the multi-purpose use of reservoirs is one of the main methods available to satisfy this demand'. Furthermore, 'as well as facilities for water-based sport, reservoirs already provide enjoyment on a large scale through their bird and fish populations, and give a no less real pleasure to countless people merely as a landscape feature'.[45]

Exaggeration and special pleading is, of course, part of the coinage of this type of verbal exchange, but clearly the arguments are by no means all on one side. The problem is essentially one of weighing them against each other in relation to particular proposals. The difficulties involved can be appreciated by studying the different positions adopted by the Water Resources Board and the Countryside Commission in relation to reservoirs in the Dartmoor National Park.[46]

Rivers and Canals

Rivers and canals are not only sources of water supply and receptacles for effluent: they are also important commercial arteries, pleasure-cruising routes, and locations for many water-based recreations. The various uses conflict and give rise to some nice problems of balancing economic and social costs and benefits. Apart from its commercial activity, the British Waterways Board is responsible for 1,400 miles of 'cruiseways', it accommodates 13,000 pleasure craft, and (on a one-day summer count) 33,000 anglers and 9,000 walkers and cyclists on the towing paths. It is estimated that a total of about half a million people are using the waterways for annual holidays, weekend recreation and frequent casual visits.[47] The areas of conflict are numerous, and some uses are incompatible (e.g. some forms of boating and angling), but given overall management and control most uses can be accommodated,[48] while at the same time provision can continue to be made for land drainage and water can be supplied in increased quantities. Shortage of finance, however, poses a perpetual problem. The Board makes an annual loss of about £2 million. Income from pleasure uses is small (£¼ million in 1970), though not as small as that of the national parks (£55,000 in 1969–70). The future of some 600 miles of waterway not designated as either 'commercial' or 'cruising' is still uncertain, though with the increasing concern for recreational planning, the great attraction of water for recreation and the large potential which exists on the waterways, it seems reasonable to hope that more and more of these 'remainder waterways' will be safeguarded.

The potential exists not only in rural areas such as the Norfolk Broads[49] but also in the heart of industrial areas such as Birmingham and the Black Country, as a recent study by Lewis Braithwaite has shown.[50]

GREEN BELTS

Green Belts around major urban areas are commonly thought of as barriers to urban growth. As such, any 'encroachment' is viewed as a planning failure. This negative role of green belts is one aspect of what would now be called regional re-structuring: a distribution of population and activities to accord with an overall physical plan aimed at producing an efficient land-use pattern and preserving areas of amenity. It necessarily implies a positive policy of catering for urban development pressures in new and expanding towns beyond the green belt. The successful achievement of such a policy depends on an adequate assessment of pressures and the allocation of sufficient land in appropriate places to cater for them. If, however, insufficient account has been taken of the pressures, if they mount to a greater extent than had been assumed, if the 'appropriate' places are for some reason or other insufficiently viable, or if the machinery of planning is not competent (e.g. because of division of responsibility) to implement all the interlocking parts of the plan, then the plan will fail at its weakest point. This is inevitably the point at

101

which the pressures are the strongest, namely in the green belt. The very fact that an area is designated as a green belt is an indication of the pressures which are bearing upon it.

Viewed thus, green belts cannot be discussed adequately except in the context of the overall plan of which they form only one part. (Some discussion is to be found in the previous chapter, in the section on 'urban policies'.) There is, however, a very different function of green belts which should be discussed here: their role in providing for the deficiency of recreational space in the urban areas which they surround.

This was the concept of the 'green girdle' which Sir Raymond Unwin put forward in his 1933 report to the Greater London Regional Planning Committee.[51] With the limited planning powers of the day this could be done only by the public acquisition of land. A scheme was devised by the London County Council under which they contributed up to half the cost incurred by local authorities in the surrounding areas in purchasing open space and farm land in order to prevent harmful development. Under this scheme (strengthened by the Green Belt Act of 1938) the L.C.C. was able before the war to secure the protection of some 25,000 acres of land, about a quarter of which is open space with full public access.

This was a notable achievement, but it was an inadequate and costly substitute for planning powers. These were provided in the early post-war legislation. It was no longer necessary to purchase land to ensure that it was retained in agricultural use: planning controls provided sufficient safeguard. Furthermore, new powers were available for obtaining public access to the countryside. It thus appeared that the vision of Abercrombie's Greater London Plan could be realized. A 'green zone' up to ten miles wide around London was proposed:

> This Green Zone is of paramount importance to London, as providing the first stretches of open country: it is here also that the public open space deficiency of the County of London will chiefly be made up; where organized large-scale games can be played, wide areas of park and woodlands enjoyed and footpaths used through the farmland. The absolute purchase of land for full public use, under the admirable Green Belt Act, should thus continue where the land is suitable for playing fields and where it consists of specially beautiful places of natural or artificial landscape; but it is hoped that land for agriculture which will comprise the greater part of the Green Belt Ring, can be safeguarded by other and equally effective methods.[52]

102

The Abercrombie Plan was endorsed by the Government in March 1946 and the green belt proposals (though amended) have in principle formed a major plank of post-war planning in the London Region. But the emphasis has been on the green belt as a negative means of control rather than as a positive means of providing for recreation. Hertfordshire has been more explicit than most: while London saw the green belt in terms of rural amenity and recreational activity, Hertfordshire saw it in terms of a barrrier to urban growth. 'Between London and Hertfordshire, therefore, there is a common purpose in the means, if not in the object.'[53]

Table 24   Green Belts, England, 1970 [58]

Green Belt	Area of approved green belts and formal submissions or accepted sketch plans, in sq. miles
Birmingham–Coventry	772
Bristol–Bath*	257
Cambridge	55
Cheltenham–Gloucester*	21
Hampshire South Coast	380
Merseyside–Manchester	380
Metropolitan*	846
Metropolitan green belt extensions	1,242
North Tyneside*	138
Nottingham–Derby	208
Oxford	134
Sheffield–Chesterfield	20
South Tyneside	14
Sunderland*	13
Stoke-on-Trent	160
West Riding	790
Wirral–Chester	110
York	65
	5,595

An asterisk denotes approved green belts. The remainder were at the 'formal submission' or 'accepted sketch plan' stage. After a sketch plan has been 'accepted' by the Department, it is formally submitted for incorporation in the Development Plan. This procedure has now been modified by the 1968 Town and Country Planning Act.

Until the advent of Duncan Sandys as Minister of Housing no formal establishment of green belts was made in the provinces. His 1955 circular [54] asked local planning authorities to consider establishing a green belt 'wherever this is desirable in order:

103

(a) to check the further growth of a large built-up area;
(b) to prevent neighbouring towns from merging into one another; or
(c) to preserve the special character of a town'.

The response of the provincial counties was eager and it was characterized by the same preoccupation with stemming urban growth. A powerful weapon was presented to authorities increasingly concerned about the growth of major cities in their areas. Political attitudes were now reinforced by a further instrument of planning orthodoxy. Little was heard of positive recreational planning in this debate.

Perhaps it was too much to expect that the traditional battle between the land-starved towns preoccupied with the need for

Table 25 *Land Use in Approved Metropolitan Green Belt, 1959–1963* [59]

	Acres	%
Total area of green belt	680,200	100·0
Towns within green belt not covered by green belt zoning	113,100	16·6
Net area covered by green belt zoning	567,100	83·4
Of which:		100·0
(a) Villages, groups of houses and land where other surface development predominates	16,600	2·9
(b) Airfields, War Department land, reservoirs, waterworks, mineral workings, tips and other land uses of a predominantly open character	28,100	5·0
(c) Institutions in extensive grounds, cemeteries, playing fields, and other land uses appropriate to the green belt	39,800	7·0
(d) Public open space	40,000	7·1
(e) Remainder (mainly agricultural land and woodland)	442,600	78·0
Areas which have been acquired, or for which financial contributions, covenants, dedication agreements or preservation orders have been made to preserve the land in its present state (included in *Net Area* above)	66,500	11·7
Of which:		
(i) Public open space	15,900	2·8
(ii) Agriculture and woodland	47,800	8·4
(iii) Other	2,800	0·5

housing sites and the counties preoccupied with stemming urban growth would be willingly enlivened by either participant by the introduction of the complicating factor of recreation. It is, however, more surprising that the 1966 White Paper, *Leisure in the Countryside* made no reference to green belts, in spite of its emphasis on the positive provision of leisure facilities at a 'convenient distance' for town dwellers. Maybe the implication was clear enough.

Be that as it may, the development of recreational planning in the green belts has come largely from the Countryside Commission (who studiously avoid the use of the term), the Regional Sports Councils, Tourists Boards, and private commercial and philanthropic interests rather than the county planning departments.[55]

Green Belts in England now cover 5,595 square miles: 11 per cent of the land area. The Metropolitan Green Belt of itself extends over 4 per cent of England. Unfortunately, the recreational pressures on the countryside are not matched by an equal documentation. Lovett's pioneer pilot study of leisure and land use in the Metropolitan Green Belt [56] has not been followed up.[57] As a result there is little possibility at present of developing recreational planning on the basis of a knowledge of the current and potential use of the green belts.

LAND FOR RECREATION [60]

As is apparent from the previous discussion, land which has recreational value cannot be nicely separated for this use. Typically it is used also for one or more other purposes—agriculture, forestry, defence, drainage, water supply and so forth. Indeed, only a small proportion of recreational land is dedicated to this single use—as with urban parks and pleasure grounds.

Recreational use is therefore characteristically a source of potential conflict with other uses. Furthermore, recreational use itself contains conflicts: anglers and speed boat enthusiasts do not make happy companions, neither do walkers and motorists, swimmers and water-skiers, bird-watchers and hunters.

Increasingly, recreational planning is concerned with the categorization and designation of land for non-conflicting uses, and the provision of 'high density recreation areas' where mass recreation can be catered for, thus not only meeting an increasing demand in a satisfactory way but also channelling it away from areas of conflict. A major stimulus to this type of strategy was provided by the 1962 American report on *Outdoor Recreation in America*.[61] In spite of that country's vast area and its apparent abundance of recreational

105

space (one-eighth of the total land area), the report pointed to the shortage of *effective* recreational land: 'acres of land and water available to the public and usable for specific types of recreation'. The great need is for recreation within or accessible from the metropolitan areas, but (as is even more the case in Britain) there are very real limits to what can be done to increase land supply for mass recreational use. The solution lies in planning the use of such land as is, or can be made, available:

> Management decisions can increase the supply of outdoor recreation resources without an increase in acreage. If a given area is transferred from low-density use emphasizing natural environment to high-density use emphasizing facilities, more recreation opportunities are made available. At the same time, intelligent concentration of use in this way can protect other natural environments by diverting mass pressures from them. . . . This is not to imply that high-density use is necessarily desirable, but only to point out that it can serve more people. In this process, however, the nature of the recreation experience is affected. A balance of all types of opportunities should be offered, and administrative decisions can manage this balance to meet changing needs.

As a guide to help policy to this end, the Commission proposed a sixfold classification of recreational uses:

Class I: High Density Recreation Areas—areas intensively developed and managed for mass use. The need for these is particularly great in locations accessible from urban areas. Development of this nature requires heavy investment in road access, parking areas, bathing beaches and marinas, swimming baths, artificial lakes, playing fields, and sanitary and eating facilities. Such areas not only meet the need for intensive use but can also afford a means of avoiding over-concentration of people in Classes III and IV areas.

Class II: General Outdoor Recreation Areas—areas subject to substantial development for a wide variety of specific recreation uses. The special feature of these areas is the capacity through development of facilities to sustain a large and varied amount of activity, such as camping, picnicking, fishing, water sports, nature walks and outdoor games. Included are parts of public parks and forests, public and commercial camping sites, picnic grounds, trailer parks, ski areas, resorts, streams, lakes, coastal areas and hunting preserves.

Class III: Natural Environment Areas—various types of areas that are suitable for recreation in a natural environment and usually in

106

combination with other uses. In contrast to Class II areas, planning and development should emphasize the natural environment rather than the provision of man-made facilities. Developments are, therefore, restricted to the provision of access roads, footpaths, and basic but not elaborate improvements necessary for camping and related activies.

Class IV: Unique Natural Areas—areas of outstanding scenic splendour, natural wonder or scientific importance. The primary management objective here is the preservation of the resources in their natural condition. Adequate access for the enjoyment and education of the public should be provided wherever consistent with the primary objective.

Class V: Primitive Areas—undisturbed roadless areas, characterized by natural, wild conditions, including 'wilderness areas'. The policy here should be to preserve the primitive condition and the isolation that qualifies it for inclusion. The avoidance of all development is the keystone of management.

Class VI: Historic and Cultural Sites—sites of major historic or cultural significance, either local, regional or national. Although these resources do not provide recreation opportunities in the usual sense, they are closely associated with vacation travel. The primary management objective should be to undertake such restoration as may be necessary, to protect them from deterioration and overuse, and to interpret their significance to the public.

This classification may not be applicable in detail to British conditions. Indeed, it may require different modifications in different regions.[62] A study of recreational resources in the Firth of Clyde Region, however, demonstrated its broad applicability.[63]

Such a strategic and positive approach to recreational planning is only just beginning to develop in Britain: even the limited promise held out by the 1966 White Paper *Leisure in the Countryside* and the Countryside Act of 1968 [64] has been seriously affected by financial restrictions.

Recreational policy since the war has had a far greater success in preserving the countryside and stemming the rising tide of recreational activity, though in recent years the mounting pressures of an increasingly mobile and motorized population has proved overwhelming. With the small resources allocated to recreational development, the majority of the effort of bodies such as the Countryside Commission has been devoted to resisting 'alien intrusions' (such as power stations and water supply projects) in national parks,

107

though the laborious success of establishing 1,400 miles of long-distance footpaths and 74,000 acres of public 'access agreements' should not go unrecorded.

In England and Wales, ten national parks and twenty-seven 'areas of outstanding natural beauty' cover 9,700 square miles or 16·7 per cent of the total land area. It is debatable how far the term 'national park' is appropriate in England and Wales. As Max Nicholson has pointed out, they are largely in private ownership and are exposed to much exploitation: 'they must therefore clearly rank as humanly modified habitats under economic uses, and as such do not qualify either by international standards or by common sense as genuine national parks'.[65]

Curiously, Scotland has no national parks. Instead, there are five large areas, termed *National Park Direction Areas* and *Areas of National Amenity* which would be national parks if legislative provision was made for them. Furthermore, over 98 per cent of the land area of Scotland has been designated as 'countryside' within the jurisdiction of the Countryside Commission for Scotland.[66]

There is regrettably little in the way of collated statistics of land use in national parks and other such areas. Even a statement of the total area of the different types of protected land is not available. Thus Sites of Special Scientific Interest and National Nature Reserves occur in national parks and areas of outstanding natural beauty. In Scotland there is considerable overlap between National Park Direction Areas and Areas of High Landscape Value; and, of course, 'countryside' includes every other protected use.

Much clearer is the increase in recreational activity and tourism, though the evidence is scattered. Recreational activity generally is expected to treble between 1970 and the end of the century, while tourism is increasing at a rate of about 12 per cent a year.[67] Nevertheless, little is known of the factors determining the scale and character of recreational demand, the future potential or the relationship between demand and 'supply', though to confound the problem it appears that the provision of well located facilities generates new demands. At the same time, much more information is needed on potential supply and the 'carrying capacity' of particular types of recreational land.[68] Such a base is essential if positive recreational planning is to be achieved. The alternative is increasing conflicts between recreational and other uses.

An inventory of coastal land uses has recently been completed by the Countryside Commission (see Table 28). This underlines the multiple use of land in areas which attract a recreational use. It also carries an important implication: the area of land available for recreational use can change as a result of land use decisions taken in relation to non-recreational uses.

Table 26 *Areas of Rural Land Available for Public Recreation, England and Wales, 1962–1963* [69]

	Acres
National Parks:	
Statutory Access Areas[a]	30,390
Nature reserves[b]	17,360
National Trust properties	264,000
Common Lands:[c]	
minimum	265,000
maximum	1,480,000
Woodland:[d]	
minimum	770,000
maximum	2,300,000
Total:	
minimum	1,367,000
maximum	4,092,000
Inland water	208,000

Notes
(a) *De facto* access is much greater than indicated by the acreage subject to formal access agreements and order. There has, however, been an increase in this acreage each year. In 1970, the total area subject to access agreements, together with land acquired for public access by local planning authorities, in national parks *and* areas of outstanding natural beauty was 73,957 acres.
(b) In 1968, there were 87 national nature reserves in England and Wales, covering 71,704 acres.
(c) It is not known to what extent the 1½ million acres of common land are available for public recreation, but the minimum is 265,000 acres: this is the acreage which was (in 1962–63) legally available.
(d) The minimum figure of 770,000 acres of woodland available for recreational use was the extent of Forestry Commission land under plantation in 1962–63. (At 31 March 1970, this had increased to 883,500 acres.) The maximum figure of 2,300,000 acres was the total woodland areas of England and Wales excluding an allowance for unplanted Forestry Commission woodland and recorded commons and National Trust properties.

Table 27 *Land in Scotland Covered by 'Planning Policy' Restraints on Development, 1966–1970* [70]

	Thousand acres	% of Total Area (19,450,000 acres)
National Park Direction Areas	1,530	7·9
Forest Parks	262	1·3
National Nature Reserves	147	0·8
Green Belts	333	1·7
Areas of High Landscape Value	5,160	26·5

109

Table 28   *The Coasts of England and Wales, 1966–1967* [71]

Total Coastline   2,742 miles
Total 'coastal belt'   1,494,653 acres

A. Developed Coastal Frontage	Existing	Proposed	Total	
			Miles	As % of coastal frontage
	miles	miles		
Substantial built-up areas	402	23	425	15·5
Industrial and commercial uses	134	23	157	5·7
Camping and caravan sites	80	25	105	3·8
Total	616	71	687	25·0

B. Protective Ownerships	Miles		Acres	
	No.	%	No.	%
National Trust	152	5·5	25,799	1·7
Forestry Commission	18	0·6	12,005	0·8
National Nature Reserves	59	2·2	12,004	0·8
Local Nature Reserves	24	0·9	4,355	0·3
Local Authority	110	4·0	25,095	1·7
Others (commons, golf courses etc.)	51	1·9	17,292	1·2
Total	414	15·1	96,550	6·5

C. Other Protective Classifications	Miles		Acres	
	No.	%	No.	%
National Parks	266	9·7	115,303	7·7
Confirmed Areas of Outstanding Natural Beauty	781	28·5	342,511	22·9
Sites of Special Scientific Interest	465	16·9	86,707	5·8
Total	1,512	55·1	544,521	36·4

D. Defence and Other Government Land	Miles		Acres	
	No.	%	No.	%
Total	134	4·9	50,331	3·4

E. Policies of Protection	Miles		Acres	
	No.	%	No.	%
Policies of protection in Development Plan	943	34·4	423,831	28·4
Other policies of protection	773	28·2	360,624	24·1
Total	1,716	62·6	784,455	52·5

NATURAL RESOURCES

Natural resources can usefully, if unusually, be divided into those which have little or no 'economic' value (of which natural beauty and wildlife are clear examples) and those which have an economic value, sometimes of huge proportions (minerals). Both illustrate in an acute way the problems of reconciling conflicting claims on the use of land.

The subject of 'nature conservation' (to use an all-embracing term) is a great deal more complex than is generally thought. It is very much more than coping with disasters such as that produced by the *Torrey Canyon*. It is nothing short of understanding the ecology of life and the delicate balances between different species, the effect of human activities on the balance of nature, and the impact of change on the living and physical environment. As such it is an enormous subject which it is impossible even to sketch here.[72] Nevertheless, its importance cannot be overestimated. Within the present narrow context, focus is placed on land use and conflicts.

Voluntary activity in nature conservation was supplemented (but not surplanted) by the establishment by Royal Charter in 1949 of a Nature Conservancy [73]—now part of the Natural Environment Research Council. Its functions are 'to provide scientific advice on the conservation and control of the natural flora and fauna of Great Britain; to establish, maintain and manage nature reserves in Great Britain, including the maintenance of physical features of scientific interest; and to develop the scientific services related thereto'.

The Conservancy is empowered to establish nature reserves, of which there were 124 in 1968, covering 257,000 acres. It is this 'land use' activity by which it is perhaps best known, but its operations are much more extensive. It has a duty to notify local planning authorities of any area which, 'not being land for the time being managed as a nature reserve, is of special interest by reason of its flora, fauna

---

Notes to Table 28

The acreages are those of the 'coastal belt', defined as all land within a line drawn one mile inland from the coast.

Since these figures were collated, three additional Areas of Outstanding Natural Beauty have been confirmed; South Hampshire Coast, Norfolk Coast and Kent Downs.

The 'other protective classifications' (part C of the Table) are, in the main, additional to the 'protective ownerships' (part B), but there is some possible overlap.

Detailed notes on the figures are to be found in the Commission's report [71].

or geological or physiographical features'. There are over two thousand of these *Sites of Special Scientific Interest* in Great Britain.

The extensive character of the threats to the natural environment is illustrated by the wide range of Acts which relate to the Conservancy's field of operations.[74] Much of its work is concerned with the giving of scientific advice: its actual powers are limited.

One of its most important functions is to 'state the case' for conservation and to ensure that planning decisions are taken with full consideration for their implication (whether adverse or beneficial) for the ecology of the countryside. The *South Hampshire Study* provides an illustration:

> The problems on the Coast created by development in the Corridor [a twelve-mile Coastal strip from Portsmouth to Southampton] would be most severe in *Langstone Harbour*. The Nature Conservancy proposed some 10 years ago that Langstone should be made a national nature reserve, but so far no decision has been taken. Farlington Marshes, reclaimed in the 18th century in the north-eastern part of the Harbour and now colonized by rare species of grasses, are botanically interesting. This is a good example, by which we might profit, of the way in which a man-made feature has actually promoted the conservation of nature. But the chief value of the Harbour to naturalists is that it supports a wide variety of birds—waders, ducks and, in winter, some 5–10% of the world's population of dark breasted Brent Geese. The birds use both Langstone and Chichester Harbours but the latter is less important to them. Any interference with Langstone would have repercussions all along the South Coast, for it forms an important link in the chain of feeding grounds along the Coast. Bird life is in fact already threatened by human activities in and around Langstone Harbour—even though at the moment it is by no means used to capacity for recreation. There is a severe dilemma here. Its resolution is not crucial to the feasibility of urban expansion in South Hampshire, but there is no doubt that, if expansion were decided upon, the studies which have already been initiated of Langstone Harbour should be intensified in order to decide which of its two great potentials—nature reserve or recreational use—should take precedence, or whether there was any possibility of combining them.[75]

Minerals [76]

Except in cases of catastrophe, conservationists have the political problem of arousing public opinion and of making explicit the dangers of ill-considered land-use changes. Mineral workings present a different problem: their effects on the landscape (if not on the ecology) are only too apparent, but the political problem is one of economic balance. Public opinion may be quickly aroused, but it has to do battle with powerful economic forces. Furthermore, 'public opinion' may well be divided if, as is often the case, one public objects to the despoilation of the landscape while another welcomes the employment which is necessary for the retention of the economic and social life of the area. Mineral workings present in a very clear way the difficult issue of balancing conflicting interests which is the essence of planning.

There are more than forty commercially useful minerals which are produced in Great Britain. Total 'consumption' is currently about four tons per head of the population each year. By the end of the century this may have risen threefold.[77]

Major parts of the economy are dependent upon mineral extraction—steel, cement, building materials, chemicals, fertilisers. Sand and gravel—the essential raw materials of the building industry—have doubled in production since the mid fifties. Chalk extraction—vital for cement production—has increased by a half. Rising demands are being experienced for aggregates (e.g. limestone, igneous rock and hard sandstones for roadstone and concrete) and for special clays such as china clay and ball clay. Advances in mining technology have made potash mining economically feasible thus holding out the promise of a new valuable export trade.[78]

Many mineral deposits are to be found in areas of high amenity and landscape value: there is thus an inevitable clash between production and amenity interests. Where a mineral is rare there may be no alternative site for extraction (though there is, of course, always the alternative of deciding that the amenity cost is so large that extraction should be prohibited).

Fullers earth (mainly composed of the mineral calcium montmorillonite) is an example of a very rare deposit, not only in this country, but in the world.[79] Its qualities are equally rare and it has many important uses in, for example, the refining and bleaching of mineral oils. More than half the national output comes from opencast workings of deposits in a small area extending for some five miles between Redhill and Godstone. The importance of these deposits is such that the line of the proposed London–Brighton motorway was planned to avoid sterilizing over a million tons of fullers earth. (A nice illustration of the positive role of planning in safeguarding mineral resources—many of which have in the past been sterilized by urban development.) The South East Joint Planning

113

Team, in its review of minerals in the South East, concluded that 'strictly limited supply and the relatively high value of this mineral demand priority for its extraction, despite possible conflicts with amenity, environment and agriculture'.

On the other hand, a proposal for development in the North York Moors National Park for the purpose of searching for natural petroleum (including gas) was rejected on the grounds that the impact on the natural beauty of the landscape would be unacceptable even on a temporary basis.[80]

The most common minerals present different problems. Though there are many workable deposits they may have large bulk (and thus high transport costs) and relatively low value—as is the case with sand and gravel (but not with special sands such as the Quartz sand to be found in the Weald). As a result, extraction is economic only at short distances from the area where they are utilized. Nevertheless, enormous demands have depleted resources in some areas (particularly in the South East) and longer hauls are now more common, the extra costs being offset to some extent by improved roads and the use of larger vehicles. The South East is, on current indications, likely to face a serious shortage in the 1980s unless extraction is permitted on land of the highest agricultural and landscape quality.[81] Higher costs for building materials implies, of course, higher building costs; the problem may well thus take the popular form of 'what increase in house prices is acceptable to safeguard amenity?' (There is the further question of whether countryside amenity may be preserved at the cost of a deterioration of housing quality.)

No two minerals present quite the same set of problems,[82] though all present some problem. Mineral workings are very difficult to reconcile with other land uses and can hardly be an addition to amenity (though their aftermath can be turned to amenity purposes—sailing lakes in wet gravel pits for instance). Surface workings are the most immediately destructive, but the land can frequently be restored. Underground works are largely hidden from sight but give rise to subsidence problems. Most mineral workings require buildings and plant which are seldom slightly and frequently noxious or noisy. Some produce enormous quantities of waste either of the well known pit heap variety or of the incredible 'science-fiction landscape' variety to be found with brickworks in Bedfordshire and china-clay workings in Cornwall. It is a happy circumstance when the holes left by quarrying can be dealt with by the disposal of the waste from other extractive works.[83] Unfortunately, the production of, for instance, pulverized fuel ash (by the Central Electricity Generating Board) has

114

a different geographic distribution from that of sand or gravel pits which are ideal repositories for such materials. The cost of long-distance transportation can be prohibitive.

Much exploitation of minerals inevitably causes a loss in amenity. Careful siting and detailed planning can reduce this to a minimum, but the fundamental issue is whether the nation (or to be precise the spokesmen for the different interests involved) values the economic production greater than it does amenity. As Bracey has bluntly put it: 'Sometimes, no basis for agreement or compromise can be found. In such cases, lines must be drawn up and battles must be fought, and they will occur frequently, and increasingly, in a country where land

Table 29   *Derelict Land in Britain, 1967* [85]

Total Derelict Land	Acres
England	93,000
Wales	20,000
Scotland	17,000
	130,000

Areas 'justifying treatment' Regions of England:	
Northern	15,074
West Midlands	9,964
North West	9,788
Yorkshire & Humberside	7,253
East Midlands	5,367
South East	3,772
South West	3,909
East Anglia	1,714
Total England	56,841
Wales	13,272
Scotland	14,000
	84,113

Table 30   *Clearance of Derelict Land in Scotland, 1971* [86]

	Progress at 31 March 1971		
	No. of schemes	Cost £m	Acres
Completed	136	3·2	1,700
In progress	52	2·2	1,500
Formally approved	23	0·4	270
Provisionally approved	64	3·1	3,880
Under consideration	23	2·4	250
Remainder		about	7,000

115

is short and subject to pressures for competing uses.'[84] Rarely is it argued (and still less rarely agreed) that the value of amenity is greater than the value of economic production.[87] There is, however, a rather different question which arises in relation to the reclamation of the legacy of dereliction. Here the issue is not complicated by arguments over the real cost of current production and use. It is no longer a question of how much consumers are prepared to pay for their building materials, their coal or their electricity. The consumption is past: the fact that previous consumers had the benefit of low prices is irrelevant. What matters now is the value placed on restoration.

This is not typically an issue of economics, but of politics. There is (generally) no market for reclaimed land. (The exception—where land is in such short supply that it becomes 'economic' to bring derelict land back into use—may increase as land pressures mount.) It may be possible to take a broad economic approach and argue that in areas where widespread dereliction is accompanied by widespread unemployment, there is an economic justification for reclamation, as did the Hunt Committee:

> Poverty in the total environment is often associated with slow economic growth and net outward migration, and is an important component of the complex of interacting factors which make it difficult for areas to recapture their former dynamism. . . . [Derelict Land] is in our view one of the outstanding examples of the way in which an unfavourable environment can depress economic opportunity.[88]

But despite the concentration of (recorded) dereliction in the development areas (76,000 acres out of a Great Britain total in 1967 of 130,000 acres),[89] much lies elsewhere, and the implied correlation between economic growth and environmental quality is a dubious one.[90]

Dubious arguments may, of course, help in the political process where the attractiveness of a case need bear little relationship to its validity. But the basic issue is that of the amount which the electorate is prepared to pay for environmental quality.[91]

RESIDENTIAL DENSITIES

The increasing land needs of a growing—and increasingly prosperous—society have led to a reappraisal of the standards of residential density. The pre-war standard for new development was frequently eight houses to the acre, though post-war densities have

116

usually been higher. In the late fifties and early sixties increasing emphasis was placed on higher densities. A Planning Bulletin of 1962 exhorted local authorities to achieve higher densities, particularly in the 'pressure areas'.[92] The aim, however, was not to obtain 'whole-sale increases at all levels of densities'. Not only was this regarded as being undesirable, it also has rapidly diminishing land savings, as Table 31 illustrates. (There is, unfortunately, a bewildering range of alternative ways of expressing densities: dwellings per acre, persons per acre, bed-spaces per acre, etc.—and, of course, the same measures in metric terms.) 'The need for, and the advantages to be gained from, increased density are greatest at the lower end of the density scale.' This is due simply to the fact that the amount of land needed for open space, schools, shops and so on increases with the number of people living in an area: an increase in the number of people on a given *housing* site thus increases the amount of land which must be reserved around it for other purposes.

Nevertheless, an increase from a low to a moderate density can achieve significant savings in land. By raising the net density from twenty-four to forty persons to the acre (i.e. from about eight to thirteen houses—which allows about 3,000 square feet of land for each house and garden), it is possible to save seventeen acres of land for every 1,000 population. This is sufficient to house another 500 people at the same density and with the same provision for open space and other uses.*

These arguments had more than the desired effect on public sector building in the sixties (aided by very large subsidies which went a considerable way towards offsetting the huge costs of very high densities). The proportion of flats in blocks of five or more storeys increased from 7 per cent in 1953–59 to 25·7 per cent in 1966, while those in blocks of fifteen storeys or more rose from 0·4 per cent to 10·4 per cent.

Increasing concern about the problems created by very high densities (financial, social, aesthetic and land-use) led to a reaction which coincidentally reached a climax at the time of the 1968 Ronan Point disaster—the partial collapse of a 22-storey block of flats in the London Borough of Newham.[93] Since then there has been a dramatic fall in the proportion of public authority dwellings in tall blocks. Nevertheless, the pressures for 'moderate' and 'moderately high' densities remain, in both the public and private sectors.

It is all too easy to become bemused by density figures, and the issue is seldom clarified by the heated arguments which are fre-

* See note to Table 31.

Table 31 *Land Needed for Housing 1,000 People at Various Densities**

Gross population density (*persons per acre*)	Net population density (*persons per acre*)	Housing land (*acres*)	Total land requirements (*acres*)	Land saving as density increases (*acres*)
20	24	42	50	
30	40	25	33	17
40	59	17	25	8
50	83	12	20	5
60	155	8·6	16·6	3·4
70	159	6·3	14·3	2·3
80	222	4·5	12·5	1·8

* 'The table excludes such land uses as industry, central business and commercial areas, railways, sewage works, etc., because these are always excluded from gross residential areas and to include them would only serve to obscure the genuine land savings made by moderate increases in net density.'

'The figures are calculated on the assumption that 1,000 people are to be housed and provided with four acres for open space and four acres for primary schools, local roads, shops, etc. Most authorities consider that four acres of open space are not really sufficient but it is as much as or more than many towns have, especially in their inner areas, and in this sense the table is more realistic than one based on optimum standards.' (MHLG, *Residential Areas: Higher Densities*, Planning Bulletin No. 2, 1962.)

Table 32 *Local Authority Dwelling Types, 1953–1970* [94]

	1953–59 %	1960–64 %	1966 %	1970 %
Houses	67·9	48·8	47·5	51·9
Flats:				
2–4 storey	25·1	31·9	26·8	38·3
5–14 storey	6·6	12·2	15·3	8·0
15 storey and over	0·4	7·0	10·4	1·8

quently to be heard between those who advocate increased space standards (i.e. lower densities) and those who advocate more 'urban' type developments (i.e. higher densities). Without entering into the finer points of the argument, a useful quotation can be given from Osborn and Whittick [95] (who maintain that the desire of an increasingly wealthy one- and two-car owning electorate is for low densities).

A maximum local density of 14 family houses a net acre (including access roads) or 15 dwellings a net acre if 5 or 10 per cent of flats

118

at 40 an acre are provided, accommodates about 45 to 50 persons a net acre. It permits of two-storey houses of about 900–1,000 sq. ft. of internal floor space, with frontages of about 20 feet, forecourts or front gardens 15 feet deep (the absolute minimum for a sense of privacy from public roads or sidewalks), back gardens 60 feet long, and road-widths of 40 feet average (leaving, if carriageways are 20 feet wide, only 10 feet each side for a 6 foot sidewalk and a grass verge). Thus the distance between facing rows of houses is 70 feet—again the minimum for privacy. A margin of about 20 per cent has to be allowed for cross-roads, gaps between ends of terraces, and minor set-backs to give agreeable variety. The use of narrower cul-de-sac roads will increase the possible depth of some front gardens (or forecourts) but cannot increase the density unless the 70-feet distance between facades is reduced. That dimension can, of course, be reduced without destroying privacy if windows are omitted on one facade of a row of houses, but this has other obvious disadvantages.

Note that at the density of 15 two-storey dwellings an acre the prevailing back garden has an area of about 1,200 sq. ft. Adding the front garden, the area is 1,500 sq. ft. The garden of a detached house of double the floor area (1,800 to 2,000 sq. ft.) at a third of the density (five an acre) is at least four times as large (6,250 to 6,500 sq. ft.).

This is part of a plea for lower densities, which analyses of social trends and aspirations support. The pressure for higher densities is (at least in suburban areas) artificially induced by the very planning machinery which should be assessing future needs. While different densities are obviously appropriate in different areas (no one would suggest building detached houses at eight to the acre in Kensington) there is sufficient visual (and unscientific!) evidence that suburban-type developments today are frequently too 'tight' to provide desirable environmental standards (for both people and their cars). Some part of the problem could be solved by more skilful design, but there is a largely unacknowledged conflict here between rising demands for personal space and planning policies aimed at conserving land. But conservation of land is not an end in itself: it is a means to providing a satisfactory total environment. To build new housing at densities which are too high to meet current needs is a sure formula for ensuring premature obsolescence. It is no answer to this to argue that land prices dictate density. On the contrary, the amount of land which is made available and the density which is laid down by planning authorities are the real determinants.

None of this is to deny the validity and acceptability of some high density developments in and around city centres and over wider areas of London. There is, however, a real danger of indiscriminately high density developments becoming obsolete and rejected prematurely. This can already be seen in the public sector where local authorities (at least outside London) are finding increasing difficulties in letting certain types of dwellings.

It would not be justifiable in the present context to develop these arguments further: sufficient has been said to demonstrate the nature of the issue (as well as one view of it).

Whether or not the arguments are accepted, an important land policy issue has been underlined: in the situation that exists in Britain, where land uses—and their intensity—are so significantly determined by administrative and politico-professional decisions (within a financial framework set by Government), it is important that planners should understand the social needs for which they are catering. A planning machine should not only overcome the deficiencies of a 'free' market: it should also take care that it is at least as responsive to total needs as the free market is to effective demand.

RESTRAINTS ON PLANNING

Land use planning is concerned with reconciling conflicting pressures on land and determining the best use of land within the restraints imposed by physical, economic, social and political factors. A number of physical factors has been selected for discussion in this chapter, while other factors are dealt with elsewhere. In practice planning operates 'at the margin'. Much of the physical pattern of land use is already determined by existing developments, past decisions and physical restraints. Though a great deal of attention is (rightly) devoted to future patterns, the room for manoeuvre is limited, though the extent of this is significantly affected by public opinion and the values which are attached to 'the environment'. Marginal decisions, however, add up to major changes. This is the rationale underlying long-term planning. Unfortunately, experience has demonstrated that long-term planning in a society subject to the current tempo of change is by no means a simple matter. This is illustrated by post-war attempts to 'solve' the problems of compensation and betterment which arise when physical planning controls are imposed on a system of individual property rights (the subject of Chapter 5); and by urban traffic policies (the subject of the following chapter).

APPENDIX: LONG-TERM POPULATION DISTRIBUTION IN GREAT
BRITAIN

Regional Population Increases and Urban Growth

Since this chapter was written, a Government study has been published of the *Long Term Population Distribution in Great Britain*.[96]
The summary chapter of this is reproduced in Volume III of this
work. Table 33 below supplements the analysis given earlier. Of particular note is the high proportion of the area of the North West
which is in urban use (26·1 per cent). This is significantly higher
than in the South East (18·2 per cent).

Over the period 1950 to 1970, the urban area of Great Britain
increased by an estimated 825,000 acres or 20·3 per cent—twice the
rate of population increase. Regional variations were marked. Population growth ranged from 1·9 per cent in Scotland to 20·6 per cent
in East Anglia, while urban growth ranged from 17·1 per cent in the
South East to 24·3 per cent in the West Midlands.

Strikingly, though they had population increases below the national average, the three northern regions of England and Scotland
and Wales all experienced urban growth rates above or around the
national average, while in the three southern regions the opposite
was the case: population growth was well above the national average,
but urban growth was below it.

Speculating on these regional differences, the Study suggests:

The relatively high rates of urban growth in the North and Wales
presumably reflect in part the building of new housing at more
spacious standards than those generally prevailing in these regions, with their large inheritance of nineteenth century development. However, a much more important element may be modern
industrial development of a land-intensive and capital-intensive
type such as the steel mills of South Wales, or the chemical and
associated industrial complex of Teeside. The relatively low growth
in the southern regions on the other hand may reflect the more
intensive use of land for housing, combined with much more
limited heavy industrial development of the kind exemplified
above. The differences may themselves result from a combination
of high land values in parts of the southern regions, especially the
South East, government regional economic and physical planning
policies, and locational advantages of the northern regions for
certain types of heavy industry. Some of these factors interact: thus
planning restrictions on development, by limiting the effective

121

Table 33 *Regional Population Increases and Urban Growth 1950–1951 to 1970*

Area	Home population 1970	Estimated urban acreage 1970	Change in urban acreage 1950–70		Change in population 1951–1970		Percentage of area in urban use	
	Nos (*thousands*)	Acres (*thousands*)	Acres (*thousands*)	% Change	Nos (*thousands*)	% Change	1950/51 %	1970 %
Northern	3,360	345	65	23·2	232	7·4	5·9	7·2
Yorkshire & Humberside	4,812	415	70	20·3	303	6·7	9·8	11·8
North West	6,789	515	95	22·6	372	5·8	21·3	26·1
East Midlands	3,363	345	65	23·2	467	16·1	9·3	11·5
West Midlands	5,178	435	85	24·3	752	17·0	10·9	13·5
East Anglia	1,673	220	35	18·9	286	20·6	6·0	7·1
South East	17,316	1,235	180	17·1	2,099	13·8	15·6	18·2
South West	3,764	475	75	18·8	516	15·9	6·8	8·1
England	46,254	3,985	670	20·2	5,028	12·2	10·3	12·4
Wales	2,734	345	60	21·1	145	5·6	5·6	6·7
England & Wales	48,988	4,330	730	20·3	5,173	11·8	9·6	11·6
Scotland	5,199	565	95	20·2	97	1·9	2·4	2·9
Great Britain	54,187	4,895	825	20·3	5,269	10·8	7·2	8·6

supply of land, further stimulate price increases which other circumstances in any case tend to foster. Much of the post-war housing which in the northern regions has taken place at spacious densities on virgin land on the periphery of towns, in the south has resulted from infilling, or redevelopment of, existing urban land: in the metropolitan region in particular, multi-storey building on redeveloped sites and the replacement of Victorian houses in large gardens by small terraces of 'town houses' have been commonplace sources of housing gains.[97]

Table 34 *Major Restraints on Development* (*thousand acres*)

	England and Wales	Scotland[a] (mainland)	Great Britain[a]
I *Urban Area 1970*	4,330	565	4,895
II *Policy restraints—*			
Conservation Areas			
1. National Parks[b]	3,366	1,530[b]	4,896
2. Forest Parks	167	262	429
3. National Nature Reserves	77	147	224
4. Areas of Outstanding Natural Beauty	2,746	—	2,746
5. Green Belts—Statutory	1,211 ⎫	333	3,989
—Non-statutory	2,445 ⎭		
6. Areas of High Landscape Value	5,974	5,160	11,134
7. Deduction for overlap of areas in II	−583	not available	
Total Conservation Areas	15,403	(7,432)[c]	(23,418)[c]
III *Physical restraint—*			
high land			
Land over 800 ft not included in II above	1,246		
Land over 600 ft		9,840[c,d]	
Deduction for overlap in II and III		−5,316	
Total actual and potential restraints	20,979	12,521	33,500
Total area	37,343	16,674[a]	54,016[a]

Notes

(a) Figures for Scotland relate to mainland and exclude inland water (covering 390,400 acres).

(b) There are no National Parks in Scotland; figures for Scotland refer to the areas proposed as National Parks in 1947 and subject to the Town and Country Planning (Scotland) National Parks Directions, 1948.

(c) Gross, without deduction for overlap.

(d) Based on material provided by Department of Geography, University of Glasgow.

The study also attempts to list and measure the main restraints on development (Table 34). Of the 54 million acres of Great Britain, 33·5 are subject to 'actual and potential restraints', though few of these are absolute. Moreover, the classification omits agriculture. The figures in the Table are subject to heavy qualification owing to the inadequacy of the available data,[98] but they illustrate in a succinct way the constrained framework within which planning must operate.

References and Further Reading

1. See L. D. Stamp, *The Land of Britain: Its Use and Misuse*, Longmans, 3rd edition, 1962.

2. See A. Coleman, 'The Second Land Use Survey: Progress and Prospects', *Geographical Journal*, Vol. 127, 1961, pp. 168–186.

3. R. H. Best and J. T. Coppock, *The Changing Use of Land in Britain*, Faber. 1962; R. H. Best, *Land for New Towns: A Study of Land Use Densities and Agricultural Displacement*, Town and Country Planning Association, 1964; R. H, Best, 'Recent Changes and Future Prospects of Land Use in England and Wales'. *Geographical Journal*, Vol. 131, 1965, pp. 1–12; R. H. Best, 'Competition for Land Between Rural and Urban Uses' in Institute of British Geographers, *Land Use and Resources: Studies in Applied Geography*, 1968; R. H. Best and A. G. Champion, 'Regional Conversions of Agricultural Land to Urban Use in England and Wales, 1945–67', Institute of British Geographers, *Transactions and Papers*, 1970, Publications No. 49.

4. R. H. Best and J. T. Coppock, *The Changing Use of Land in Britain*, Faber, 1962, p. 229.

5. Ministry of Agriculture, Fisheries and Food, *A Century of Agricultural Statistics, Great Britain 1866–1966*, HMSO, 1968.

6. R. H. Best and A. G. Champion, 'Regional Conversions of Agricultural Land to Urban Use in England and Wales, 1945–67', Institute of British Geographers, *Transactions and Papers*, 1970, Publication No. 49.

7. See D. E. C. Willatts, 'Post-War Development: The Location of Major Projects in England and Wales', *Chartered Surveyor*, Vol. 94, 1962, pp. 356–363.

8. The Central Urban Region consists of the counties of Cheshire, Derby, Durham, Gloucester, Lancashire, Leicester, Nottingham, Stafford, Warwick, Worcester and the West Riding; and the Welsh counties of Flint, Glamorgan and Monmouth. The London Region consists of Bedford, Berkshire, Buckingham, Essex, Hampshire and the Isle of Wight, Hertford, Kent, Greater London, Surrey, East and West Sussex.

9. See reference 6.

10. MHLG, *Settlement in the Countryside: A Planning Method*, Planning Bulletin 8, HMSO, 1967. The distant areas include much of central and west Wales, limited parts of south west, northern and north west England, a small segment of country around the Wash, and the extremity of Kent.

11. Select Committee on Scottish Affairs, Session 1970–71, *Land Resource Use*, Minutes of Evidence, HMSO, H.C. 503, 1971.

12. Ibid., p. 46.

13. Ibid., p. 47.

14. Ibid., p. 14.

15. Ibid., p. 57.

16. J. Turner, 'A Statement on the Use of Agricultural Land for Housing', *National Housing and Town Planning Council Year Book*, 1953.

17. R. Gasson, 'The Challenge to British Farming 1960–1970', *Westminister Bank Review*, May 1966, pp. 32–41.

18. Net output is not a very satisfactory index of physical productivity, since varying combinations of inputs can result in differences in net output without any changes in physical yield. For fuller discussion see R. Gasson, ibid.; G. P. Wibberley, *Agriculture and Urban Growth*, Michael Joseph, 1959; Department of Education and Science, *Report of the Land Use Study Group: Forestry, Agriculture and the Multiple Use of Rural Land*, HMSO, 1966; and A. Edwards, 'Land Requirements for United Kingdom Agriculture by the Year 2000', *Town and Country Planning*, Vol. 37, March 1969, pp. 108–115.

19. J. T. Ward, 'The Siting of Urban Development on Agricultural Land', *Journal of Agricultural Economics*, Vol. 12, December, 1957, pp. 451–466. See also G. P. Wibberley, 'Agriculture and Land Use Planning', in *Land Use in an Urban Environment*, Liverpool University Press, 1961, and the same author's *Agriculture and Urban Growth*, Michael Joseph, 1960 and 'Land Scarcity in Britain', *Journal of the Town Planning Institute*, Vol. 53, No. 4, April 1967.

20. Strategic Plan for the South East, *Studies, Vol. 2: Social and Environmental Aspects*, HMSO, 1961, para. 4.30.

21. *Annual Abstract of Statistics*, 1970, Table 214.

22. Cmd. 6447, HMSO, 1943.

23. See Forestry Committee of Great Britain, *The Case for Forestry*, 1971.

24. Department of Education and Science, *Report of the Land Use Study Group: Forestry, Agriculture and the Multiple Use of Rural Land*, HMSO, 1966.

25. Neither is it technically a Forest Park: it is administered under special legislation which defines the rights of commoners and the powers of the ancient Verderers Court.

26. *Hansard*, 24th July, 1963, Cols. 1467–1472.

27. *Forty-eighth Annual Report of the Forestry Commission, 1966–67*, H.C. 311, HMSO, July, 1968, p. 10.

28. Sylvia Crowe, authoress of *Forestry in the Landscape*, significantly published by the Forestry Commission (Booklet No. 18, HMSO, 1966).

29. *Forty-ninth Annual Report of the Forestry Commission, 1967–69*, H.C. 171, HMSO, February, 1970, p. 13.

30. Estimated figures, including New Forest.

31. See V. Bonham Carter, *The Survival of the English Countryside*, Hodder & Stoughton, 1971, especially pp. 182 ff.

32. It should be stressed that this only touches a highly complex issue. For further discussion see R. H. Best and J. T. Coppock, op. cit.; G. P. Wibberley, op. cit., and *Report of the Land Use Study Group*, op. cit.

33. Highlands and Islands Development Board, *Fifth Report 1970*, HMSO, 1971, p. 49. See also, Natural Resources (Technical) Committee, *Forestry, Agriculture and Marginal Land*, HMSO, 1957.

34. *Taken for Granted: Report of the Working Party on Sewage Disposal*, HMSO, 1970, p. 2 (based on estimates by the Water Resources Board).

35. *The Future Management of Water in England and Wales* (Wilson Report), HMSO, 1971, p. 6. In relation to Scotland see Scottish Development Department, *Local Government Reform: The Water Service in Scotland* (Taylor Report), HMSO, 1972.

125

36. Wilson Report, op. cit., p. 94.
37. J. Wreford Watson and J. B. Sissons, *The British Isles: A Systematic Geography*, Nelson, 1964, p. 86.
38. Wilson Report, op. cit., p. 7.
39. Ibid.
40. *Taken for Granted: Report of the Working Party on Sewage Disposal*, HMSO, 1970.
41. V. Bonham Carter, *The Survival of the English Countryside*, Hodder & Stoughton, 1971, p. 183.
42. See 'Note on Difficulties over the Building of New Reservoirs', in *The Future Management of Water in England and Wales*, HMSO, 1971, pp. 99–100, from which the quotations are taken.
43. See Water Resources Board, *Water Supplies in South England*, HMSO, 1966; *Interim Report on Water Resources in the North*, HMSO, 1967; *Report on Desalination*, HMSO, 1969; 'Future Patterns of Development' in *Seventh Annual Report of the Water Resources Board* (1969–1970), HMSO, 1971, pp. 64–71; and *Water Resources in the North*, HMSO, 1970.
44. Council for the Protection of Rural England, *Annual Report 1969*, pp. 13–14.
45. See also Central Council for Physical Recreation, *Inland Waters and Recreation*, 1964.
46. See particularly, *Fifth Annual Report of the Water Resources Board* (1967–68), HMSO, 1968, Appendix C ('Water for Plymouth'); *Second Report of the Countryside Commission* (1968–1969), HMSO, 1969, pp. 33–36 and *Third Report of the Countryside Commission* (1969–1970), HMSO, 1970, Appendix C ('Plymouth and South West Devon Water Bill'), pp. 61–63 and also pp. 42–44.
47. British Waterways Board, *Annual Report, 1970*, HMSO, 1971, p. 8.
48. See *Report on Broadland* by the Nature Conservancy (1965): 'The problems arising from the incompatibility of certain users in Broadland could be eased by the introduction of a system whereby activities which tend to conflict are separated from one another geographically or in time or both' (p. 57).
49. The Nature Conservancy, *Report on Broadland*, 1965.
50. Lewis Braithwaite, *The Use of Urban Canals*, Centre for Urban and Regional Studies, University of Birmingham, 1970.
51. For a fuller discussion see London County Council, *Green Belt Around London*, 1956, and David Thomas, *London's Green Belt*, Faber, 1970, Chapter 3.
52. P. Abercrombie, *Greater London Plan*, HMSO, 1945.
53. Hertfordshire County Council, *Report on the Administrative Problems of the Green Belt*, 1957, p. 4.
54. *Green Belts*, MHLG Circular No. 42/55, HMSO, 1955. See also D. Mandelker, *Green Belts and Urban Growth*, University of Wisconsin Press, 1962, p. 30.
55. And the bigger cities themselves: see Greater London Development Plan, *Report of Studies*, GLC, 1969, Chapter 5. Mention should also be made of the Lee Valley Regional Park Authority established by special legislation; see *Lee Valley Regional Park*, published by the Authority in 1969.
56. W. F. B. Lovett, 'Leisure and Land Use in the Metropolitan Green Belt', *Journal of the Town Planning Institute*, Vol. XLVIII, No. 6, June 1962, pp. 150–157.
57. But see D. Thomas, op. cit., pp. 196 ff, and Greater London Council, *Surveys of the Use of Open Space*, GLC, 1968 and *Greater London Development Plan: Report of Studies*, GLC, 1969, Chapter 5.
58. MHLG, *Handbook of Statistics 1970*, HMSO, 1971, Table 36.
59. Strategic Plan for the South East, *Studies Vol. 2: Social and Environmental Aspects*, HMSO, 1971, p. 182.

THE PHYSICAL FRAMEWORK

60. For further discussion see the author's *Town and Country Planning in Britain*, Allen & Unwin, 4th edition, 1972, Chapter IX.

61. *Outdoor Recreation in America: A Report to the President and to Congress by the Outdoor Recreation Resources Review Commission*, U.S. Government Printing Office, Washington D.C., 1962.

62. Note also Max Nicholson's statement that 'it is still unclear how far quite different types of areas under different management are needed to satisfy the varied needs for conservation of natural environment and wild life, scientific studies in natural conditions, preservation of fine scenery and landscape, tourism, education, enjoyment of wilderness, maintenance of forest reserves and provision for outdoor sports and recreation'. *The Environmental Revolution*, Hodder & Stoughton, 1970, p. 127.

63. *Recreation Planning for the Clyde*, Scottish Tourist Board, 1970.

64. *Leisure in the Countryside: England and Wales*, Cmnd. 2928, HMSO, 1966. The Countryside Act of 1968 extended the responsibilities of the National Parks Commission and reconstituted it as the Countryside Commission. A Scottish Act provided for the establishment of a Countryside Commission for Scotland: there has previously been no Scottish equivalent to the English legislation on National Parks and Access to the Countryside.

65. Max Nicholson, *The Environmental Revolution*, Hodder & Stoughton, 1970, p. 127.

66. The source for this statement is *Britain 1971*, HMSO, 1971, p. 176.

67. Select Committee on Scottish Affairs, op. cit., p. 49.

68. This is defined as 'the level of recreation use an area can sustain without an unacceptable degree of deterioration of the character and quality of the resource or of the recreation experience'. (Countryside Commission, Countryside Recreation Glossary.) For a discussion of research needs, see Countryside Recreation Research Advisory Group, *Research Priorities*, Countryside Commission, 1971.

69. T. L. Burton and G. P. Wibberley, *Outdoor Recreation in the British Countryside*, Wye College, 1963, p. 8.

70, Select Committee on Scottish Affairs, Session 1970–71, *Land Resource Use*, H.C. 503, 1971, p. 57.

71. Countryside Commission, *The Coasts of England and Wales: Measurements of Use, Protection and Development*, HMSO, 1968.

72. See Max Nicholson, *The Environmental Revolution*, Hodder & Stoughton, 1970, and the references quoted therein.

73. See *The Nature Conservancy Handbook 1968*, HMSO, 1968 and *The Nature Conservancy: Progress 1964–1968*, HMSO, 1968. An earlier examination of the work of the Nature Conservancy is to be found in the *Seventh Report from the Select Committee on Estimates*, Session 1957–58, H.C. 255, HMSO, 1958.

74. Cf. the Electricity Act, 1957, which provides:

In formulating or considering any proposals relating to the functions of the Generating Board or of any of the Area Boards . . . the Boards in question, the Electricity Council and the Minister, having regard to the desirability of preserving natural beauty, of conserving flora, fauna and geological or physiographical features of special interest, and of protecting buildings and other objects of architectural or historic interest, shall each take into account any effect which the proposals would have on the natural beauty of the countryside or on any such flora, fauna, features, buildings or objects.

75. *South Hampshire Study: Report on the Feasibility of Major Urban Growth*, HMSO, 1966, para. 43, p. 20. See also Strategic Plan for the South East, *Studies*

Vol. 2: Social and Environmental Aspects, HMSO, 1971, Chapter 6, 'Conservation and Environmental Resources'.

76. For a fuller discussion of the machinery of planning in relation to the control of mineral workings and the safeguarding of mineral deposits see the author's *Town and Country Planning in Britain*, Chapter VIII.

77. Strategic Plan for the South East, *Studies Vol. 2: Social and Environmental Aspects*, HMSO, 1971, para. 5.1, p. 90.

78. A new series of 'dossiers' collating factual information on mineral resources is being published by the Mineral Resources Consultative Committee: see *Mineral Dossier No. 1: Fluorspar*, HMSO, 1971.

79. Strategic Plan for the South East, op. cit., p. 100.

80. See *Report of the Ministry of Housing and Local Government 1969 and 1970*, Cmnd. 4753, HMSO, 1971, p. 29.

81. See *Strategic Plan for the South East: Report*, HMSO, 1970, pp. 34–35 and *Studies, Vol. 2*, loc. cit.

82. See *Town and Country Planning 1943–1951 Progress Report*, Cmnd. 8204, HMSO, 1951, Chapter VII.

83. See J. C. Wylie, *Progress in Refuse Disposal*, Council for the Preservation of Rural England, Sheffield and Peak District Branch, 1962; E. G. Barber, *Win Back The Acres*, Central Electricity Generating Board, 1963; and John Barr, *Derelict Britain*, Penguin Books, 1969, pp. 167–170.

84. H. E. Bracey, *Industry and the Countryside*, Faber, 1963, p. 199.

85. Few statistics are available on the extent and location of derelict land (but see reference 91). The figures are taken from the Hunt Report on *The Intermediate Areas*, Cmnd. 3998, HMSO, 1969, pp. 28–29. No indication is given of the criteria for 'justifying treatment'.

86. Select Committee on Scottish Affairs, Session 1970–71, *Land Resource Use*, p. 50, para. 52 and p. 59.

87. E. J. Mishan is the outstanding exception: see his *The Costs of Economic Growth*, Staples Press, 1967 and the 'more popular version', *Growth: The Price We Pay*, Staples Press, 1969.

88. *The Intermediate Areas*, Cmnd. 3998, HMSO, 1969, para. 29 and 457.

89. Ibid., para. 75.

90. See the Note of Dissent to the Hunt Report by Professor A. J. Brown, op. cit., p. 155 et seq. and, for a much broader approach, E. J. Mishan, op. cit.

91. In Circular 4/71, the DOE requested local planning authorities in England to carry out a survey of derelict land in their areas. The results of this survey are summarized below. The first column shows the acreage of land dealt with in 1970; the second, the total amount of derelict land on 31 December 1970; the

Derelict Land Survey 1970 (England)

Region	Acreage restored in 1970	Dereliction at 31.12.70	Acreage justifying restoration	Acreage to be restored in 1971
N.W.	288	14,767	11,995	939
N.	762	20,864	15,366	1,759
Y. & H.	856	12,384	8,967	1,070
E.M.	461	8,792	7,319	840
W.M.	824	11,936	9,998	939
S.W.	129	19,026	3,574	132
E.A.	43	3,333	2,507	40
S.E.	282	5,595	3,309	451
England	3,645	96,697	63,035	6,170

third, the amount considered to justify restoration; and the fourth, the amount which local authorities expected to be restored in 1971.

Analysis of Derelict Land at 31.12.70

	Acres
Spoil heaps	35,530
Excavations and pits	23,093
Other forms of dereliction	38,074
Total	96,697

92. MHLG, *Residential Areas: Higher Densities*, Planning Bulletin No. 2, HMSO, 1962, (from which the quotations are taken).

93. MHLG, *Report of the Inquiry into the Collapse of Flats at Ronan Point, Canning Town*, HMSO, 1968.

94. *Housing Statistics, Great Britain*, No. 24, February 1972, Tables 10 and 12.

95. F. J. Osborn and A. Whittick, *The New Towns: The Answer to Megalopolis*, Leonard Hill, revised edition, 1969, pp. 123–124.

96. DOE, *Long Term Population Distribution in Great Britain: A Study*, HMSO, 1971.

97. Ibid., p. 53.

98. Ibid. Appendix 8.

Chapter 4

Traffic in Towns[1]

No apology is needed for taking the title of the Buchanan Report [2] as the title for this chapter. It remains the most relevant and thorough survey of the problems posed by the motor car in urban areas. This chapter is concerned in the main only with traffic in urban areas. This is not to deny the importance of inter-urban traffic planning. Indeed this is crucially important to the solution of urban traffic problems. But traffic *between* towns gives rise to few problems which cannot be solved by expenditure on road building and landscaping. The first 1,000 miles of the motorway network are now complete and a further 1,000 miles are planned for completion by the early 1980s. Following the publication of a 'green paper' in 1969 [3] the next stage of the inter-urban road plan was announced in June 1971.[4] The main aims of this are:

(i) to achieve environmental improvements by diverting long-distance traffic, and particularly heavy goods vehicles, from a large number of towns and villages, so as to relieve them of the noise, dirt and danger which they suffer at present;

(ii) to complete by the early 1980s a comprehensive network of strategic trunk routes to promote economic growth;

(iii) to link the more remote and less prosperous regions with this new national network;

(iv) to ensure that every major city and town with a population of more than 250,000 will be directly connected to the strategic network and that all with a population of more than 80,000 will be within 10 miles of it;

(v) to design the network so that it serves all major ports and airports, including the new Third London Airport at Foulness; and

(vi) to relieve as many historic towns as possible of through trunk road traffic.

Such a policy will, in time, solve most of the problems of inter-urban traffic (the exceptions include weekend holiday traffic congestion which is probably an insoluble problem). Intra-urban traffic problems are a very different matter. It is these which forcibly demonstrate that the motor car is a 'mixed blessing' (to borrow the title of an earlier book by Buchanan).[5] As a highly convenient means of personal transport it cannot (at present) be bettered. But its mass use restricts its benefits to car users, imposes severe penalties (in congestion, pollution and reduction of public transport) on non-motorists, involves huge expenditures on roads, and at worst plays havoc with the urban environment.

The starting point is the enormous growth in road vehicles: from 2·3 million in 1940, to 9·4 million in 1960, and to nearly 15 million in 1970 (Table 35). Over the twelve years 1957 to 1969, the number of passenger miles travelling by private transport increased threefold, from nearly 60 to 184 thousand million miles (Table 36). Car users are obviously prepared to pay heavily for personalized transport: the amount of expenditure has increased *pari passu* with the increased ownership and use of cars, and the proportion of total consumers' expenditure on private cars has also increased—from 2 per cent in 1951 to 8·5 per cent in 1970 (Table 37). At the latter date expenditure on the purchase and running of motor vehicles totalled £2,659 million (producing a tax revenue of over £1,000 million).

Car-owners use their cars for a multiplicity of purposes. The acquisition of a car is also the acquisition of mobility. Not only are trips previously made by public transport now made by car, but additional trips are made which would not be made at all without a car. The pattern of car trips is complex (as any transportation study convincingly demonstrates). Though popular attention tends to be focused on the flood of cars to central business districts, this is only one aspect of the problem. Moreover, since most trips to central business districts are in fact made by public transport it is not the most important aspect. Indeed, by parking restraints in the central area it is perhaps one of the easier aspects to be dealt with. Trips to

Table 35 *Motor Vehicles Licensed, Great Britain, 1904–1970* [6]

	Private cars and vans	Motor cycles, scooters and mopeds	Public transport vehicles	Goods vehicles	Total (including other categories)
		Thousands			
1904	8		5	4	18
1920	187	288	75	101	650
1940	1,423	278	81	444	2,325
1960	5,526	1,796	93	1,397	9,439
1965	8,917	1,612	96	1,600	12,938
1970	11,515	1,048	103	1,616	14,950

work in total are a different matter, since in any city jobs are located over a wide area and, while efficient mass transit systems are viable to a central point, they are much more difficult to organize to dispersed locations. This issue is of such importance as to warrant more extended discussion.

Table 36   *Passenger-Miles by Various Means of Transport, Great Britain, 1952–1969* [7]

Thousand million passenger miles

	Road		Rail	Air*	Total
Year	Public service vehicles	Private transport			
1952	50·1	37·9	24·1	0·1	112·2
1957	45·9	59·9	25·9	0·3	132·0
1962	42·4	107·1	22·8	0·7	173·0
1967	37·0	167·9	21·2	1·2	227·3
1969	35·7	184·0	21·6	1·2	242·5

* Including N. Ireland and Channel Islands.

Table 37   *Consumers' Expenditure on Motor Vehicles, 1951–1970* [8]

Expenditure on Motor Vehicles as % of Total Consumers' Expenditure	1951	1961	1970	1970 Actual Expenditure £m
Purchase	0·7	2·8	3·1	980
Running costs	1·3	2·9	5·4	1,679
Total	2·0	5·7	8·5	2,659

JOURNEYS TO WORK

The great growth in personal mobility stimulated by increases in real incomes and made possible by the development, first of public transport and later of private transport has very considerably extended the range of choice in both jobs and houses. In any given residential area this increased mobility has given households a much wider field of employment opportunities. Similarly, employees of any particular firm now have a much wider field of housing opportunities. It is important to stress these positive advantages since so much of the debate on journeys to work is couched in terms of 'problems'. There is, however, no denying that these exist: in some areas on a very large scale. The increased separation of homes and jobs can lead to problems of peak-hour congestion, of uneconomic transport investment, of employment difficulties for secondary

132

earners (particularly housewives) and of the sheer strain and fatigue of travel.

Transport has become (and is now recognized as being) a crucial element in land-use planning. Transport facilities have a major impact on land use, while land uses have important traffic generating effects. Transport is, indeed, the life blood of modern industrial society. (Significantly, urban transport problems are often popularly referred to as constituting 'thrombosis'.) Though the journey to work is by no means the only problem-creating element, it is one of the most important.

It is useful to draw a distinction between 'journey to work' and 'commuting': the former relating to all home-to-work journeys, the latter to the mass movement to a central work place. If people move out of cities to suburban locations and continue to work in the central area, commuting increases. If jobs move out as well, commuting may actually decrease. But in both cases there will still be a journey to work. The distinction is important, since the major transportation problem is essentially that of providing for commuters. (It should be pointed out, however, that the distinction is not widely made: the two terms are frequently used interchangeably.)

Most figures on journey to work are taken from successive census volumes. These demonstrate both the increase in the number of journeys and the increase in the distance travelled. In 1966 the proportion of the economically active in employment* who worked outside the area of the local authority in which they lived was 34 per cent in England as a whole (excluding Greater London). The 1921 proportion was 21 per cent. Journeys from rural districts increased even more markedly: from 22 to 47 per cent. Journeys from rural districts into towns increased fourfold, from 387,000 to 1,495,700.[9]

All such figures, however, suffer from the fact that they relate to administrative areas. Since the number of rural districts decreased by about a quarter between 1921 and 1966 and there were also very large boundary extensions (which added a quarter to the total urban acreage), they understate the scale of the change. If local government is reorganized into much larger units the statistical trend will be reversed! The figures, therefore, simply indicate the trend: they are not very useful for measuring it. An adequate analysis of the changing patterns of journey to work require much more sophisticated data—which is one reason for the large number of transportation studies which have been carried out in recent years.

* i.e. excluding the unemployed and those with no fixed workplace or who did not state their workplace.

Patterns of journey to work are made up of three elements: the location of jobs, the location of homes, and the means of transport. Unfortunately, though there is an enormous amount of statistics on each of these, they are not generally produced in a form which allows the patterns to be established.

Only rarely are employment and housing neatly concentrated in self-contained areas. (Aycliffe is one of the rare exceptions—with a major employment centre located on the site of a wartime ordnance factory alongside the new town.) Though there are local centres of manufacturing employment in 'industrial estates', and ubiquitous 'housing estates' throughout the country, the pattern of journey to work is typically very complex. The complexity has been increased by the growth of service employment which now constitutes a half of the total. Furthermore, much modern manufacturing industry is not tied to specific locations. As the studies undertaken by the South East

Table 38   *Travel to Work in Central London by Area of Residence, 1966* [10]

| Area of residence | Area of workplace | | | |
	Central area	Rest of Inner London	Outer London	Total
Central London	111,400	16,120	4,320	131,840
Rest of Inner London	521,070	803,230	140,810	1,465,110
Outer London	481,130	253,590	1,575,520	2,310,240
Total Greater London	1,113,600	1,072,940	1,720,650	3,907,190
Outer Metropolitan Area	191,750	43,660	164,960	400,370
Outer South East	27,030	5,820	7,690	40,540
Total	1,332,380	1,122,420	1,893,300	4,348,100

Joint Planning Team pointed out, 'journey to work studies using "centre-place" concepts and employment catchment areas are to some degree an academic rationalization by planners, economists, traffic engineers, etc. for their own purposes. Patterns of movement to individual work places are necessarily a complex overlapping of individual movements which reflect a choice of homes in relation to jobs or vice versa.'[11]

Nevertheless, in general, two clear patterns emerge: first, the great majority of work trips are short-distance; secondly, this basic pattern is overlain, in the large urban areas, by commuting to the centre. The former tends to be overshadowed by the latter. Even in

134

London (in 1964), a half of journeys were of less than 4 miles [12] and the average journey length (in 1962) to jobs outside the central area was only 2·6–2·8 miles.[13]

Central London is, of course, unique. In its ten square miles it employs 1,332,000 workers. By no means, however, do the majority of these have a long journey to work (in terms of mileage): 11,000 or nearly 9 per cent live in the central area and a further 521,000 (nearly 40 per cent) live in the rest of Inner London. Rather more than a half travel in from Outer London Boroughs and beyond— 219,000 (16 per cent) from outside Greater London. The majority (90 per cent) of those working in Central London travel by public transport. Those travelling by car come predominantly from Inner London.

The study of *North-East London* carried out for the Greater London Council by Buchanan [14] stressed the extreme complexity of the movement of people (and goods) throughout London. 'Local centres and widely dispersed elements generate strong cross-currents. It is essential to appreciate the scale of this complexity if one is to make any positive step toward easing the problems of movement in London, and it is important to divest oneself of the notion that the whole cause of traffic congestion is a tide of private cars flowing into and within Central London.'

Nevertheless, 'taken in all its forms—from private cars to buses and trucks, the motor vehicle is clearly the mainstay of transport in London'. And, though improvements in other forms of transport are not beyond the bounds of possibility, it is not possible to envisage the motor car being supplanted in the forseeable future.[15] 'The fact of the matter is that the motor vehicle with its ability to provide a door-to-door service is a highly convenient and useful method of transport. It is very difficult to visualize a substitute offering the same advantages which is not in effect a motor vehicle.'

URBAN ROAD NETWORKS

The implication, however, is not that nothing can be done to reduce congestion, noise and 'the brutal injuries that motor traffic inflicts on the urban environment'. On the contrary, it is that a road network has to be provided which will carry the amount of traffic which cannot be restrained. Like the better known Buchanan Report on *Traffic in Towns*, there is little examination in the N.E. London Study of the potentialities for restraint (by some pricing mechanism, for example). There is thus the danger (which is acknowledged) that additional roads will simply attract additional traffic. Nevertheless,

135

some restraint—other than that created by congestion—is accepted as being inevitable. Yet the issue then becomes one of public acceptability, and the opinion is given that 'there is as yet no indication in London or elsewhere that heavy degrees of restraint are practicable in terms of the feasibility of providing an acceptable standard of service with alternative modes of transport'.

The degree of restraint which is practicable is very much a matter of argument (to which we shall return). Buchanan maintains, however, that the only practicable solution to the problem of 'reconciling the pressures for greater mobility with the demand for a better environment' necessarily involves the provision of a primary network of major roads (as far as possible purpose-built motorways) supported by a 'secondary network possessing a pronounced hierarchical structure'. The latter, in essence, is the improvement of existing roads to take greater (but differing) amounts of traffic. These roads would be selected on the basis of their relationship to the primary roads (particularly to interchange points) and local environmental factors.

This was essentially a (qualified) support for the London 'ringway' system which has attracted such fierce opposition. (The qualifications related to the total design of motorways and the environmental and social factors which needed to be—expensively!—taken into account.) The case for the primary network was that it would 'contribute substantially to the more efficient circulation of London's traffic, especially of commercial and industrial vehicles: if accompanied by appropriate policies for environmental management and the development of a supporting network, it can provide a framework for the re-ordering of many of the commercial and industrial activities of London'.

So fierce, however, has been the opposition to urban motorways in London (particularly after the experience of the impact of Westway) that Buchanan felt it necessary to set out the argument against the 'No Motorways Alternative'. The short answer was that the real choice was not between motorways and no motorways, but between having traffic choked on existing streets (with disastrous environmental effects) and having it 'partly on existing streets and partly on a new network'.

The arguments employed in *Traffic in Towns* were reproduced. It is worth quoting this section in full since it clearly highlights the crucial elements of the problem:

In [*Traffic in Towns*] three main variables were postulated in connection with urban traffic: the standard of accessibility (or degree of usage of motor vehicles), the standard of environment (or degree of freedom from the adverse effects of motor traffic), and the extent of physical alterations (and hence of capital expenditure) for the purpose of accommodating motor traffic. It was pointed out that any urban community faced with traffic problems can play these variables in a number of ways. If it seeks the usage of a great deal of traffic and insists at the same time on high standards of environment then it must be prepared to spend a great deal of money on effecting the necessary physical changes (new road networks, parking places, etc.). If it is not prepared to spend any money, or a minimal sum at most, then it can still have good environmental conditions provided it suppresses the traffic or most of it. If it is unwilling to spend any money yet desires a great deal of traffic, then it can achieve these objectives by letting the environment go to rack and ruin.

In practice, however, the options are not as wide open as these examples suggest. Whatever may have happened to date, no responsible authority could now say that it proposed to disregard environmental standards. Nor could any authority say that it intends to suppress all traffic, for even if it chose to take a very tough line with the use of private cars for commuting journeys to work and for pleasure, it would soon find that there is a rock-bottom volume of traffic associated with commerce and industry which cannot be suppressed if life is to go on. Moreover, whilst tough measures may be feasible against cars used for commuting in circumstances where alternative methods of transport either exist or can be contrived, there is nothing on the scene to suggest that people are likely to be deterred from using their cars for a great many social journeys for which there is no form of transport providing anything remotely resembling the convenience of the car.[16]

Buchanan sets out his judgements (and it is important to be aware that this is what they are) in a plausible and convincing way. But elegance of exposition must not blind the reader to the unproven and tendentious basis of the argument (and, indeed, of alternative arguments). In truth, little is known of the acceptability or effectiveness of measures of traffic constraint nor, indeed, how far improved roads merely generate additional traffic and thus defeat their ostensible purpose.

Yet another Buchanan Report, on roads in the Greenwich–Blackheath area,[17] demonstrates a shift in emphasis: 'It is perfectly clear that, in the case of London and all other large cities, the

137

objectives must be to transfer to public transport as much of the total demand for movement as is reasonably possible.' Nevertheless, the major problem is seen to be that of persuading the commuter to Central London to abandon his car in favour of public transport. Yet this has already been shown to be only a small part of the problem since so many such commuters already use public transport.

A major part of the problem lies with vast numbers of car journeys which Buchanan describes in almost lyrical terms: 'There are an immense number and variety of personal and social journeys made in our cities that extend and enrich people's lives, and for which the private car offers a more versatile medium than public transport.'

While accepting the essential validity of this (with the qualification that when too many try to enrich their lives in this way, the result is far from enrichment, not only for the motorist but also for the non-motorist) no attempt is made to examine how far restraint is practicable, nor how far the provision of additional roads actually exacerbates the very problems they are intended to solve.

The assumption is that the 'primary network' will channel off traffic from existing secondary roads and 'environmental areas', but it can equally well be argued that every improvement merely attracts more traffic. Indeed, one can go further and argue that the extra traffic generated by urban motorways could result in a greater congestion on the roads which feed them.[18]

An objective observer might comment that convincing proof of either proposition is lacking. Nevertheless, American experience provides good grounds for arguing that road improvements are self-defeating: 'The greater the expenditures have been, the greater has become the need. With it all, no city can say, regardless of how much it has poured into providing conveniences for its motorists, that it does not have far more congestion and far greater inconvenience than when it embarked on its costly venture.'[19]

Transportation studies have become increasingly sophisticated (and expensive), but none has adequately demonstrated where the best balance between road improvements and public transport improvement lies.

TRAFFIC AND THE ENVIRONMENT

The Buchanan approach implies that there is some minimum level of private transportation for which roads must be built. An alternative is to take the urban environment (to which, to be fair, Buchanan attaches much—even if insufficient—importance) as the starting

138

point. The *Greenwich and Blackheath Study* provides a good basis for developing this approach. Twelve tests are proposed for judging the possible impact of road alignments:[20]

Impact on People's Lives
1. Number of households to be displaced;
2. Conditions of dwellings to be demolished;
3. Length of residence of households to be displaced;
4. Loss of schools and number of schoolchildren to be affected;
5. Loss of shops and disturbance to shopping;
6. Severance of 'cohesive areas';
7. Loss of open space;
8. Loss of jobs through the demolition of industrial and office premises;

Impact on Environment
9. Noise;
10. Visual impact;
11. Loss of buildings of quality;
12. Present use and total area of land needed.

These criteria are, with currently available techniques, crude and (perhaps inevitably) usable only in a subjective way. Indeed, it is highly doubtful whether 'scientific' measures of level of acceptability are possible, but this applies equally to measures of the public acceptability of 'restraint' (by way, for example, of parking and pricing measures). Thus the issue is revealed for what it truly is: one of judgement to be decided by political pressures. The jargon of the transport planner (with modal splits, gravity models and the like) serves to confuse the issues and represents an attempt (even if unintentional) to replace political judgements by pseudo-professional technics.

If 'sufficient' expenditure were incurred on the urban road programme in conjunction with a major programme of urban renewal and with great improvements in public transport, it might be possible to be less worried about the impact of road plans. It is, however, impossible to have confidence that 'sufficient' expenditure will, or can be, incurred. The Greenwich–Blackheath Study demonstrated that 'extraordinary measures would be required to ensure that the new network did not do irreparable harm to highly valued areas of historic and architectural interest'.[21] The London motorway proposals as a whole are estimated to displace some 90,000 people.[22] Can the displacement of such a number of people (a very small minority of the total population of London, but nevertheless a significant absolute number) be justified for the benefit of the majority?

There must be serious doubts and these are clearly shared by Buchanan, as is clear from his remarkable paper, *The Price of Posterity:*

> So many lessons have been learned in recent years regarding the design of urban motorways, including many learned by painful experience in the U.S., that given the resources there would be no difficulty in designing the network in such a way that once built its adverse effects in the way of noise, and disruption would be absolutely minimal . . . (but) I wish I had more confidence that in redeveloping such a huge place as London we had the ability to do the job properly. . . . We have allowed the vital overhaul of road systems to lag far, far behind everything else. In many instances the work has got so far behind that the opportunities for overhaul had been fatally prejudiced by other redevelopments, and the task made infinitely more difficult, more expensive, and productive of greater hardship.[23]

Buchanan's doubts are widely shared. Given the huge cost of the London primary road network (possibly £2,000 million) [24] it does not seem conceivable that the additional expenditure required 'to accommodate the motorways in a successful manner' will be forthcoming. Nor does it seem likely that, if such levels of expenditure on roads were attained, they would be accompanied by adequate expenditure on public transport.

The public reaction to the completion of the £33 million Westway has highlighted the basic message of Buchanan's work: to accommodate large numbers of cars in urban areas in a civilized manner involves a very high level of expenditure. If this level is unacceptably high, a lower level will suffice only if there are fewer cars. In essence, therefore, the issue is one of restraining the use of cars to the level which can be satisfactorily accommodated within the urban fabric.

This means that there has to be some form of rationing. The Crowther Report (which prefaced *Traffic in Towns*) argued that severe limitations on the use of cars in towns would be almost impossible to enforce, even if a car-owning electorate were prepared to accept such limitations in principle. But that was ten years ago, since when an additional five million cars have appeared on the roads of Britain. Public attitudes to the rationing of road space are undoubtedly changing.[25] It is in this context that pricing techniques need to be considered.

ROAD PRICING

The total amount of 'car taxes' paid by motorists is a nice subject for endless debate. However, the issue of concern in the present context is the way in which this total (whatever it may be) is levied. The importance of this can be illustrated by taking extreme examples. First, all the tax could be raised by way of a purchase tax: this would have the effect of discouraging the purchase of cars, but once purchased there would be no disincentive to their use either generally or in areas of congestion. Secondly, all the tax could be raised by a fuel tax: the effect would be a high rate of car-ownership but a restraint on the general use of cars. Thirdly, all the tax could be raised by tolls on the use of roads. If applied generally, this would have a similar effect to a heavy fuel tax (though it would be more expensive to administer). If applied at different rates to different roads, the use of some roads (e.g. in central urban regions) could be discouraged while the use of others (e.g. by-passes) could be encouraged.

Examples could easily be multiplied, but the point is sufficiently clear: the way in which cars are used can be crucially affected by the way in which taxes are levied. Of course, the matter is not a simple one: much depends on alternative methods of transport, the taxes (or subsidies) which they bear, and the extent to which they provide a service which is equivalent to that of the motor car. Without entering into the complexities to which these wider issues give rise, it is obvious that (theoretically at least) an alternative to adapting towns to cars is to adapt the use of cars to the capacity (however defined) of town roads.

Yet a further alternative is to do neither, and to allow 'natural' congestion to determine the extent to which cars and roads are used.

In a car-owning democracy such extremes are beyond the bounds of public acceptability. Practicable alternatives lie, not at the extremes, but at some compromise point between the extremes. Moreover, any given situation is compromised by past policies. The motor car allows and encourages a wide dispersion of homes and jobs (in the same way as the development of public transport caused 'corridor' development along the new lines of rapid communication). Once this dispersal has taken place it is not easy (or even desirable) to reverse it.

Nevertheless, the area for choice in public policies is substantial. Emphasis can be placed on providing better roads along which the motorist can travel, and parking spaces at which he can stop; or emphasis can be placed on improving public transport and restricting car use. There is no easy technical or political formula for deciding where the emphasis should lie (or, to be more realistic, where the

141

balance between the alternatives should be struck). It is here that road pricing policies are of particular relevance.

In Britain these have now been accepted for parking and, to a much more limited extent, on certain short stretches of very high cost roads (the Severn and Forth Bridges for example). The former are intended (and operate) as a form of rationing while the latter are intended as a means of recouping a proportion of the cost of provision. (The levels at which they are set have only minimal rationing effects.)

Parking controls are discussed further in a later section: here we need to discuss at greater length the potential for rationing the use of roads by the price mechanism.[26]

There are obvious differences between the economics of car production and the economics of road production. The car producer aims to meet only those 'needs' for which there is a demand at a price sufficient to enable him to make a profit. The 'road producer' has no such clear-cut objective. He can attempt to estimate current needs and to predict future needs, but he has no ready-to-hand formula for assessing the relationship between costs and benefits (despite the growth of cost–benefit analysis). Moreover, while the supply of cars can be increased (or reduced) in relation to effective demand, 'road supply' is a matter for political decision. The amount of road space can be increased only slowly; but the use of roads can change dramatically.

The car user is unconcerned with the cost of providing roads: so far as he is concerned (virtually) all roads are a 'free' public service for which he pays very indirectly through taxes. The only direct cost which is related to his use of roads is the fuel tax. This does not increase in relation to the increased cost of new roads. On the contrary, on uncongested new roads he will probably be able to use his fuel more efficiently and thus pay less fuel tax; but the marginal difference is small.

There is a nice contrast with the telephone user. Like roads, telephones are a public service, but telephone charges vary according to demand, with increased rates at peak periods. This has the effect (or at least the objective) of restraining demand at these periods. Those who judge that they must make a telephone call in the peak period pay the increased charge; others use the off-peak period. The 'peak' is thus reduced to manageable proportions.

Car-users, on the other hand, do not typically have a choice as to the time at which they make their journeys: their choice is between using their personal car and using public transport. Since the personal car is—to the individual—frequently so much more convenient

142

and comfortable than public transport, a car owner will use his car unless restraints are imposed. Car-parking restrictions are one such restraint, but theoretically there are many others, apart from congestion itself which in extreme conditions—as in Central London—operates as a restraint. (The level of restraint imposed, however, imposes severe penalties on other road users, such as buses and commercial transport.)

These alternatives include purely administrative measures (e.g. permits to use particular roads or to bring a car into defined areas) and 'admission charges' or tolls. Such measures would be difficult (and costly) to administer, and the evidence suggests that they are impracticable.[27] Apart from parking controls (to which we return in the following section) the only alternative restraint is some system of direct charging for the use of roads. To date, however, no practicable scheme has been devised. The problem lies in the range of features which a scheme must have. The Smeed Committee[28] listed nine important and eight desirable requirements of a pricing system:

Most Important Requirements

(1) Charges should be closely related to the amount of use made of the roads (either in terms of time or distance).
(2) It should be possible to vary prices to some extent for different roads (or areas), at different times of day, week or year, and for different classes of vehicle.
(3) Prices should be stable and readily ascertainable by road users before they embark upon a journey.
(4) Payment in advance should be possible, although credit facilities may also be permissible under certain conditions.
(5) The incidence of the system upon individual road users should be accepted as fair.
(6) The method should be simple for road users to understand.
(7) Any equipment used should possess a high degree of reliability.
(8) It should be reasonably free from the possibility of fraud and evasion, both deliberate and unintentional.
(9) It should be capable of being applied, if necessary, to the whole country and to a vehicle population expected to rise to over 30 million.

Desirable Requirements

(10) Payment should be possible in small amounts and at fairly frequent intervals, say amounts not exceeding £5 and intervals

143

not exceeding one month. This does not exclude payment in larger amounts where preferred.

(11) Drivers in high-cost areas should be made aware of the rate they are incurring.

(12) At the same time the attention of drivers should not be unduly diverted from their other responsibilities.

(13) The method should be applicable without difficulty to road users entering from abroad.

(14) Enforcement measures should impose as little extra work on the police forces as possible and should therefore lie within the capacity of traffic wardens.

(15) It would be preferable if the method could also be used for street parking.

(16) The method should, if possible, indicate the strength of demand for roadspace in different places so as to give guidance to the planning of new road improvements.

(17) The method should be amenable to gradual introduction commencing with an experimental phase.

Any method of pricing which meets these requirements involves some type of meter. Two main systems are possible: 'point pricing' and 'continuous pricing'. Under the first, a meter would be fixed to the vehicle (similar to a taxi-meter). Charges could be paid in advance for a fixed number of times when the vehicle passes a pricing point. Alternatively, remote control units could 'read' vehicles passing a price point: charges would be made in a manner similar to that used for telephones.

Either of these methods could also be used for the second type of system, under which vehicles would be charged according to the length of time or distance travelled in a metered zone. (This might be compared with the STD system for telephone charging.)

It is not clear at the present time whether some such system would be practicable. The Ministry of Transport 1967 study of *Better Use of Town Roads* was not in a position to decide, but had no hesitation in stating that it was potentially the most efficient means of restraining traffic.

It should perhaps be made clear that, though road pricing would have implications for motor taxation policy, its particular purpose is to restrain the use of cars in pre-determined areas. There is no reason why all the tax revenue which it is intended to raise from motorists should not be collected in this way, but this is a logically (if not politically) separate issue.

PARKING CONTROLS

It is clear that road pricing is for the future. In the meantime, the best means of restraint is clearly by way of parking controls. Here the car commuter is of particular importance since he accounts for a significant proportion of peak hour congestion. (Though the proportion of *people* who commute by car varies between different towns, in all cases commuters' *cars* contribute disproportionately to congestion.)

'Free' or 'cheap' parking is such only in a limited sense of the terms. It is uneconomic in that it leads to a wasteful use of space and those who are prepared to pay for it are penalized in comparison with those who are prepared to cruise around or queue until space can be obtained; it encourages long-term parking and thus benefits the commuter (who has the alternative of public transport at least in the final stages of his journey) as against those (e.g. commercial travellers) who must use their cars; it discourages the provision of car parks; it encourages traffic congestion and reduces the efficiency (and increases the costs) of bus services. In these and similar ways it shields the car user from the real cost of his motoring and imposes costs which are met by others. What is 'free' or 'cheap' to the individual motorist is not so on a broader analysis.

Since the possibilities of increasing on-street parking spaces is minimal (and, more typically, a negative quantity because much of it needs to be prohibited in order that streets can be used more effectively by moving vehicles), charges for parking are not only a rationing device, but also a means by which the economic demand for off-street parking can be measured and met.

Parking controls thus have objectives other than that of simply discouraging excessive use of cars for journeys that could be made by public transport. Whatever the 'appropriate' level of road use by moving vehicles some system is needed to meet the economic demand for parking (and thus for determining which road users shall be able to park).

Theoretically the upper limit to parking provision should be set by the capacity of the roads (as judged in a broad context, including environmental considerations). Without a pricing system for the *use* of roads this limit can in fact be lower than the limit judged on purely parking-capacity grounds. If a motorist bears no direct cost for using congested roads he will be prepared to pay more for parking than he would if he had to pay for the total cost of both moving and parking. (Hence the superiority of a charging system which relates to the time spent in a priced area over one which relates to the distance travelled within the area.)

145

It was confusion on this point that led to planning requirements for the provision of private parking space in new buildings. Conceived as a means of ensuring that new buildings should 'consume their own smoke', it is now seen as having serious limitations. It exerts control only at the date of redevelopment: yet the pace, scale and location of redevelopment bears no necessary relationship to the rate of traffic growth, the demand for parking provision, or the capacity of the adjacent roads to carry the traffic. It is inflexible, costly to developers, and constitutes an unjustified subsidy (at private expense) to a restricted group of parkers.

It is now officially accepted (by the central government if not by all local authorities) that such 'non-operational' parking provision (i.e. parking which is not necessary to the operation of the business of particular buildings) should be limited and, more important, planned as a part of a comprehensive parking policy.[29] In turn, parking policy needs to be related to transportation and land use plans for urban areas as a whole.

In discussions of parking controls much is made of the distinction between 'essential' and 'non-essential' or 'optional' traffic (similar to the distinction between operational and non-operational traffic). This goes back at least as far as *Traffic in Towns*, but it lies deep in planning philosophy. In the Glossary to *Traffic in Towns*,[30] the terms are defined:

Essential traffic is the business, commercial and industrial traffic which is necessary to serve and maintain the life of a community. *Optional traffic* is the traffic arising from the exercise of a choice to use a vehicle for a journey when the option existed either not to make the journey at all or to make it by some other kind of vehicle or form of transport. Bus traffic may be regarded as essential to the extent that buses are essential to carry loads which for various reasons cannot be discharged by individual cars. There is not necessarily always a very clear distinction between the two. Some apparently essential trips may, upon examination, prove less essential than some optional trips. In addition, if the distinction is made between the two at *peak periods*, some commercial trips could be called optional, in that they could be made at some other time of day.

This classification has had rough treatment from economists.[31] Quite apart from its confusion between a classification by selected activities and a classification by substitutability, it is difficult to see how it can be utilized. Again the superiority of a pricing system is manifest.

146

Though the object of fierce controversy when they were introduced, parking meters are now accepted as part of the urban way of life. Increased charges and differential charges (high in the central area, lower in adjacent areas) has made them increasingly effective and they have certainly contributed to the improved speed of movement in London [32] and elsewhere. Many of the problems to which they give rise result from the policy of emphasizing their *rationing* function rather than their *pricing* function.[33] Meter charges are often too low: this is evidenced by the number of motorists cruising around to find spaces (thus adding to the congestion which meters are intended to reduce). The rationing emphasis is clearly illustrated by the time-limits imposed. The justification for this is taken to be the need to discriminate against long-term parkers in favour of those wanting space for a short time. This is thought to be 'fairer'. A Ministry of Transport report, for example, states that 'it is better—in the general interest—for eight vehicles to be able to use a street parking space in a day than for one to occupy it all day'.[34] Roth nicely shows that this is by no means self-evident.[35] 'Do we say that it is in the general interest for seven people to be able to stay at a hotel for one night each rather for one person to stay a whole week?'

The essence of the matter, however, is that it is difficult to determine an appropriate charge for car-parking in congested areas while ever there is no charge for car-moving in such areas.

GOODS TRAFFIC

So far in this chapter, attention has been restricted to passenger transport. Yet over one-third of the traffic throughout the day in Central London (and nearly a quarter of peak-hour traffic) is goods traffic.[36] Most roads goods traffic is short-distance: 70 per cent of all roads goods tonnage is hauled twenty-five miles or less; only 6 per cent travels a hundred miles or more.[37] In short, most goods traffic originates and ends within relatively small urban regions. The scope for diverting goods traffic away from major urban areas is thus restricted. Diverting goods from lorries to trains would similarly be of small effect (quite apart from any economic implications) since the final stages of the journey would still need to be by road.

Road pricing is as relevant to goods traffic as it is to passenger traffic, though the economic effects are more problematic (an issue to which we return at the end of this chapter). In the absence of this, emphasis is placed on loading and unloading controls, and on minimizing the impact of goods traffic on the environment by way of, e.g. lorry routes and lorry parks.

147

Of particular concern is the increase in the number of 'heavy' goods vehicles. These are officially defined as those of over three tons unladen weight. The number of these nearly doubled in the sixties to around 420,000. But the increase in larger lorries has been more dramatic: those over eight tons increased from 11,000 to 55,000 between 1960 and 1970.[38]

Containerization and the increased size of lorries, coinciding with a mounting public concern for environmental quality, has led at one and the same time to a new problem and to a rapid recognition of it. Vehicles designed to transport large loads efficiently on a motorway become totally unacceptable 'alien intrusions' in towns designed for a very different system of transport. A report by the Civic Trust listed over forty 'categories of nuisance' created by a vehicle which is quite out-of-scale: a bull in a china shop, to use the phrase of Tony Aldhous.[39] These categories included noise, damage to buildings, accidents, parking nuisance, danger and visual intrusion.

Current road building policies will result in a major part of heavy traffic by-passing free-standing towns.* Noise can be reduced by the production of quieter vehicles and stricter enforcement of measures to keep them quiet.[40] Indeed, given sufficient public concern (which is clearly increasing) and an adequate planning framework, many of the problems can be significantly mitigated. The necessity for an adequate planning framework can be illustrated by reference to lorry parks.

Lorry Parks

Lorry parks are a nice example of the need for positive planning. The public sector is concerned about the destructive effect of lorry parking on amenity, but has been reluctant to use local ratepayers' money to meet a problem which is caused largely by non-ratepayers, and which, in any case, cannot be solved by individual authorities acting independently. Lorry parks need to be provided in accordance with a co-ordinated national plan on the basis of the major transport routes. Haphazard provision could lead to expensive over-provision in some areas and inadequate provision in others. Moreover, the public sector (currently at least) lacks the expertise needed for the provision and operation of a commercial venture of this type.

On the other hand, the private sector lacks the power to acquire appropriate sites for this purpose—'appropriate' in the sense of being sited so as to fit in with the need for a rational distribution of parks in locations which meet planning and amenity requirements. As with

* See above, p. 130.

public sector enterprise, private enterprise could lead to an uneven distribution of parks unrelated to wider needs. Furthermore, appropriate sites may be prohibitively costly. Yet, given the necessary planning framework, allocation of sites, and (where necessary) the compulsory acquisition of land, private enterprise has the expertise, the capital and the incentive to operate lorry parks.

It was for these reasons that the Bennett Committee on Parking of Lorries [41] concluded that the provision of purpose-built lorry parks should be a co-operative venture between public and private enterprise:

This could be done by the authority associating itself with a commercial organization to the extent that the authority, after agreeing with the local planning and/or traffic authority (where these are different) provides the land, if necessary using its compulsory powers for the purpose, and subsequently leases it to a private developer to build and operate the lorry park. We are of the opinion that, in the present circumstances, it is only by means of such a partnership that a national chain of lorry parks of the sort we are proposing will become a reality.[42]

PUBLIC TRANSPORT

The importance of public transport varies between different towns, largely in relation to size. Broadly speaking, the larger the city the greater is the proportion of commuters who use public transport. Given current (and increasing) rates of car-ownership, the superiority of the private car to the individual traveller, and the low direct costs borne by the motorist for using his car in urban areas, this is to a significant extent a result of congestion. It is just not possible for all who would like to use their cars for travelling to central areas to do so. Improved roads, however, remove some of the constraints—until a new level of congestion is reached.

In this battle for space, public transport suffers. There is the familiar cycle of congestion leading to higher costs, higher fares, poorer service and declining custom. In this downward spiral those who use (whether by necessity or by choice) public transport are penalized.

Public transport is, nevertheless, a highly efficient means of conveying large numbers of passengers to 'nodal points'. This is particularly the case with 'fixed-track' systems such as railways. Buses have the advantage of making very economical use of road space and are much more flexible. (One-day censuses carried out in London in 1970 revealed that of the road vehicles and passengers entering

149

Central London in the morning peak, 3,900 buses carried 150,900 passengers while 73,600 cars brought in only 103,000 passengers.) [43] Neither can rival the extreme flexibility of the motor car (though new types of transport might), but the motor car cannot be accommodated in sufficient numbers to dispense with the need for public transport. Moreover, those who cannot afford, or, for some reason or the other, are unable to drive cars increasingly suffer as measures are taken to adapt to a high level of car ownership and use. The elderly in particular rely on public transport and are severely affected when its service is drastically reduced.[44]

Even in the U.S.A. about a fifth of households do not have cars: a proportion which rises significantly for those living in central cities, the poor and the elderly.

The fundamental issue is that, for those who have cars, the advantages of travelling by car involve very similar financial costs irrespective of the costs imposed on other road users. 'Cheap' public transport is likely to have little effect on the relativities. Even 'free' fares would not tempt many motorists (as the Rome experiment with the no-fare bus suggested). It is not the high cost of public transport which makes people use cars: it is the low cost and attractiveness of car travel. Parking controls have reduced these attractions: road pricing would reduce them further.

Paradoxically, schemes of 'traffic management', designed to ease the flow of traffic, have frequently benefited the motorist but not the public transport passenger: for him bus stops are increasingly inconvenient. Recent pilot schemes with bus-only lanes and the

Table 39   *Proportion of Households in the U.S.A. Without Cars, 1960 and 1967* [45]

	1960 %	1967 %
Area:		
United States	25	21
SMSA*		
Central cities	38	32
Fringe	18	13
Outside SMSA	20	18
Annual income:		
Under $3,000	56	57
$3,000 to $9,999	13	14
$10,000 plus	5	4
Age of head of household:		
Under 65 years	20	16
Over 65 years	50	44

* Standard Metropolitan Statistical Areas.

'contra-flow' bus lane in Piccadilly have, as yet, done little to correct the balance. Where extensive schemes of this type have been implemented, however, the public response has been positive. In Reading, for example, a network of contra-flow bus lanes and bus-only streets (which has reduced journey times by up to 50 per cent within the area of the scheme) has resulted in an increase in the number of passengers—reversing a decline which was continuous over the previous five years.[46] The planning of bus services in conjunction with new development (as in Runcorn New Town) [47] or redevelopment (as in Leeds) [48] offers the greatest scope for spectacularly increasing the attractiveness of public transport.

Development of public transport services is, of course, expensive and the case for subsidies is a strong one (at least until the time when the motorist bears the proper cost of his journeys). This is now accepted and the Transport Act of 1968 provides an extensive system of grant-aid. It also provided for the establishment of Passenger Transport Authorities in areas where it is particularly important to have 'integrated' plans for public transport. These measures are discussed elsewhere,[49] as are the new type development plans which deal not only with broad land-use policies but also with policies for integrating land-use and transport planning, and policies for traffic management.[50]

LAND USE AND TRAFFIC

Traffic is a function of land use, and thus planning policies and decisions relating to land use have important traffic implications. The greater is the amount of 'dormitory' development on the periphery of towns, for example, the greater is the amount of commuting to places of work. Over a longer period, the congestion created by this commuting may be one of the factors leading to the dispersal of employment. The forces for dispersal (of both homes and jobs) are themselves affected by available transport systems. The development of public transport in the late nineteenth and early twentieth centuries led to radial growth along the new lines of communication. Later, the motor car allowed an unprecedented freedom of movement and gave rise to a rapid rate of urban growth of an amorphous character.

The freedom of location (for both homes and jobs) has led to a very complex pattern of urban functions which in turn has resulted in extremely complex travel patterns. Commuting from suburban homes to central area jobs is only a small part of the overall pattern. Moreover, though many office jobs have been created in recent

151

years in central areas, manufacturing industry, warehousing and distribution have increasingly decentralized.

Mounting emphasis on relating physical planning and transportation policies is the logical response to this. In London, for example:

> The general policy of seeking to encourage development around certain focal points on the rail system, with easy accessibility and adequate interchange facilities, is already being pursued. It is now proposed, in particular, that the Council shall encourage the concentration of offices and other developments on or around Underground stations outside the central area. In this way some measure of reverse-flow commuting will be possible and employers can be helped to attract employees from a wider area.[51]

Larger questions, at least for London and the other—much smaller—conurbations, relate to future urban form and size. The long-standing British policy of restraining urban growth embraces a physical concept of the city which the accessibility provided by the car outdates. *Traffic in Towns* extols the virtues of 'compactness' ('which seems to contribute so much to the variety and richness of urban life') and warns against the dangers of 'sprawl' (defined as 'dispersal . . . taken beyond a certain point').[52] 'Sprawl', however, is an emotive term, not an operational concept. Given the demand for car-ownership and use, increasing 'dispersal' seems inevitable, while increasing dispersal itself is a factor in the rising demand for cars. In truth, the choice is between relatively high densities and 'compactness', accompanied by a low rate of car ownership and use on the one hand, and lower densities, dispersal and a high rate of car ownership and use on the other hand. One cannot have it both ways: as *Traffic in Towns* assumes.[53] Major urban motorway plans take many years to implement. During this period many of the activities which they are intended to serve may disperse though, in the British context, planning controls may retard or even prevent some of this dispersal (e.g. hypermarkets in semi-rural locations). What will in fact happen cannot be predicted (though the building of urban motorways will undoubtedly have a significant influence). But towns as we know them can continue to exist only if they are adequately serviced by public transport and if private car use is severely restrained.

Yet it is unwise to be dogmatic. It may be unpopular to espouse the cause of 'incremental' planning (and by implication to deny the validity of 'comprehensive' planning). Nevertheless, the difficulty of prediction, together with the very long period of time which is needed to implement a comprehensive plan, strongly urges caution.

References and Further Reading

1. See also Volume III of this work, Chapter 8: J. M. Thomson, *Half-way to a Motorised Society*.

2. Ministry of Transport, *Traffic in Towns*, HMSO, 1963. A shortened (and much more easily handled) version was published by Penguin Books in 1964. This edition, however, omits two useful appendices: 'The Environmental Capacity of Streets', and 'Cost–benefit Analysis and Accessibility and Environment'.

3. Ministry of Transport, *Roads for the Future: A New Inter-Urban Plan*, HMSO, 1969.

4. See *Roads in England 1971*, H.C. 74, HMSO, 1972, Chapter 2, from which the quotation is taken.

5. C. D. Buchanan, *Mixed Blessing: The Motor in Britain*, Leonard Hill, 1958.

6. DOE, *Highway Statistics 1970*, HMSO, 1971, Table 2.

7. *Passenger Transport in Great Britain 1969*, HMSO, 1971.

8. Central Statistical Office, *Social Trends*, No. 2, 1971, HMSO, 1971. Tables 36 and 37.

9. Royal Commission on Local Government in England, Volume III, *Research Appendices*, Cmnd. 4040–II, HMSO, 1969, pp. 25–26.

10. South East Joint Planning Team, *Studies Vol. I: Population and Employment*, HMSO, 1971, Table 6.1, p. 242.

11. Ibid., para. 6.5.

12. *National Travel Survey*, 1964.

13. Greater London Development Plan, *Report of Studies*, Table 6.13, p. 163. The detailed figures are:

Area of Employment	Mean Work Journey Length (miles)
Central area	6·2
Inner London (excluding central area)	2·8
Remainder of LTS area	2·6
Total London Traffic Survey Area	3·7

14. Colin Buchanan and Partners, *North East London: Some Implications of the Greater London Development Plan*, GLC, 1970. The quotations are from this Report and the separately published *Summary*.

15. See also Ministry of Transport, *Cars for Cities*, HMSO, 1967.

16. *North East Lonodon*, op. cit., para. 197, pp. 92–93.

17. Colin Buchanan and Partners, *Greenwich and Blackheath Study*, GLC, 1971.

18. See, for example, J. M. Thomson, *Motorways in London*, Duckworth, 1969, Chapter 4.

19. G. W. Anderson, 'Urban Mass Transportation' quoted in Political and Economic Planning, *Solving Traffic Problems—I: Lessons from America*, PEP Planning Broadsheet No. 402, 1956.

20. *Greenwich and Blackheath Study*, op. cit., Appendix 4, 'Appraisal of the Various Alternative Alignments for the South Cross Route of Ringway I'.

21. C. Buchanan, *The Price of Posterity*, British Road Federation, 1972.

22. *Ibid*. None too convincingly, Buchanan suggests that, of these 90,000 people, the number who will feel themselves grievously affected would be around 30,000.

23. Ibid.

24. J. M. Thomson, op. cit., p. 142.
25. The 1968 White Paper, *Transport in London* (Cmnd. 3686, HMSO) could say quite blandly (as could not have been said a decade earlier) that 'the control of traffic must be regarded as a deliberate part of highway and transport planning. In many cases regulation is appropriate. But the price mechanism is often more flexible and more sensitive. It may in time prove possible and worthwhile to reflect in charging systems the costs which journeys on overcrowded roads impose on other road users.'
26. There is a growing literature on this subject. Four particularly useful references are:

(a) Ministry of Transport, *Road Pricing: The Economic and Technical Possibilities* (Smeed Report), HMSO, 1964.
(b) Ministry of Transport, *Better Use of Town Roads*, HMSO, 1967.
(c) G. Roth, *Paying for Roads: The Economics of Traffic Congestion*, Penguin Books, 1967.
(d) J. M. W. Stewart, *A Pricing System for Roads*, University of Glasgow, Social and Economic Studies, Occasional Papers No. 4, Oliver & Boyd, 1965.

27. See *Better Use of Town Roads*, op. cit.
28. *Road Pricing*, op. cit., pp. 7–8.
29. MHLG, *Parking in Town Centres*, Planning Bulletin 7, HMSO, 1965. See also Ministry of Transport, *Traffic and Transport Plans*, Roads Circular No. 1/68, HMSO, 1968.
30. Ministry of Transport, *Traffic in Towns*, HMSO, 1963, p. 222.
32. See, for example, M. E. Beesley and J. F. Kain, 'Urban Form, Car Ownership and Public Policy: An Appraisal of *Traffic in Towns*', *Urban Studies*, Vol. 1, No. 2, November 1964, pp. 174–203; D. J. Reynolds, *Economics, Town Planning and Traffic*, Institute of Economic Affairs, 1966, especially pp. 94–96; G. Roth, *Paying for Parking*, Institute of Economic Affairs, 1965 and *Paying for Roads: The Economics of Traffic Congestion*, Penguin Books, 1967.
32. See Greater London Council, *The Effectiveness of Parking Control as a Means of Traffic Restraint*, Greater London Development Plan Inquiry Paper B.479, July 1971.
33. G. Roth, *Paying for Roads*, op. cit., p. 108.
34. Ministry of Transport, *Parking—The Next Stage*, HMSO, 1963.
35. G. Roth, op. cit., p. 101.
36. Ministry of Transport, *Better Use of Town Roads*, HMSO, 1967, p. 14.
37. Ibid., p. 16.
38. DOE, *Highway Statistics* 1970, Table 6.
39. See T. Aldhous, *Battle for the Environment*, Fontana, 1972, p. 55. Chapter 4 of this book, 'Lorries in Towns', gives a summary of the Civic Trust report.
40. See Noise Advisory Council, *Traffic Noise: The Vehicle Regulations and their Enforcement*, HMSO, 1972.
41. DOE, *Lorry Parking: The Report of the Working Party on Parking of Lorries*, HMSO, 1971.
42. Ibid., para. 2.5.
43. GLC, *Report of the Policy and Resources Committee*, 23 June 1971.
44. See *Age Concern on Transport*, National Old People's Welfare Council, 1971.
45. T. H. Floyd, quoted in M. M. Webber and S. Angel, 'The Social Context for Transport Policy', U.S. Panel on Science and Technology, Tenth Meeting.

Science and Technology and the Cities, U.S. House of Representatives, U.S. Government Printing Office, 1969, p. 109.

46. DOE Traffic Advisory Unit, *Comprehensive Traffic Management in Reading*, DOE, 1972.

47. Runcorn is developing a bus-only trackway system serving the whole town. See Runcorn New Town Development Corporation, *Runcorn New Town—Draft Plan*, 1965, Chapter 12.

48. See *Planning and Transport—The Leeds Approach*, HMSO, 1969.

49. J. B. Cullingworth, *Town and Country Planning in Britain*, Allen & Unwin, 4th edition, 1972, pp. 108–112.

50. Ibid., p. 99 et seq.

51. GLC, *Report of the Policy and Resources Committee*, 23 June 1971.

52. *Traffic in Towns*, op. cit., p. 31, paragraphs 61–62.

53. On this see M. E. Beesley and J. F. Kain, op. cit., p. 185. ('It is quite wrong to assume, as the Report does, that Great Britain will have future levels of car ownership and use equal to those in the United States at comparable levels of income, and at the same time to argue that it will possess fundamentally different urban areas. . . .')

Chapter 5

A Note on Land Values[1]

LAND CONTROLS AND VALUES

Land use planning in Britain developed from the public health and housing policies introduced in the nineteenth century to deal with the problems of 'the health of towns'. Individual property rights were restricted in the interests of public health: owners were statutorily required, for example, to maintain their properties in good sanitary condition; new buildings had to conform to certain building standards; minimum street widths were laid down. It was accepted that these restrictions were necessary in the public interest and that owners should be compelled to comply without the right to any compensation. At the extreme, owners of houses which were 'unfit for human habitation' could be compelled to demolish them without recompense.

However, it is one matter to require an owner to comply with the law relating to public health: it is a very different matter to require him to comply with planning schemes designed to safeguard agricultural land, to ensure that urban growth is restrained or to protect or enhance amenity. Early planning legislation safeguarded the position of owners: if restrictions reduced the value of land, compensation was payable; and the amount of compensation was determined in relation to the most profitable use of the land, even if it was unlikely that the land would be so developed. Furthermore, no regard could be had to the fact that the prohibition of development on one site could result in a shift of the 'development value' to another site. Each piece of land was valued separately and the owner given 'full' compensation, with little concern for the desirability to the community of the restrictions being imposed and their effect on other land.[2]

This highlights the crucial issue of land use planning in a society in which individual ownership is an established and accepted institution: 'at what point does the public interest become such that a private individual ought to be called on to comply, at his own cost, with a restriction or requirement designed to secure that public interest?'.[3]

156

There are, however, additional complications. Planning set out to achieve a selection of the most suitable pieces of land for particular uses. Some land will, therefore, be zoned for a use which is profitable for the owner, whereas other land will be zoned for a use having a low—or even nil—private value. It is this difficulty of 'development value' which raises the compensation problem in its most acute form. The development value which may legitimately—or hopefully—be expected by owners is, in fact, spread over a far larger area than is likely to be developed. This potential development value is, therefore, speculative, but until the individual owners are proved to be wrong in their assessments (and how can this be done?) all owners of land having a potential value can make a case for compensation on the assumption that their particular pieces of land would, in fact, be chosen for development if planning restrictions were not imposed. Yet this 'floating value' might never have settled on their land, and obviously the aggregate of the values claimed by the individual owners is likely to be greatly in excess of a total valuation of all the pieces of land. As Haar has nicely put it, the situation is akin to that of a sweepstake: a single ticket fetches much more than its mathematically calculated value, for the simple reason that the grand prize may fall on any one holder.[4]

Furthermore, the public control of land use necessarily involves the shifting of land values from certain pieces of land to other pieces: the value of some land is decreased, while that of other land is increased. In other words, planning controls do not necessarily destroy land values: they typically result in their shifting to another site.

Yet to the individual owner this is of no concern: a restriction on the use of land deprives him of a potential value. The fact that a neighbour may be given permission to develop adjacent land (and benefit from the consequent increase in realizable value) is hardly likely to make him feel less aggrieved.

In theory it is logical to balance the compensation paid to aggrieved owners by collecting a betterment charge on owners who benefit from planning controls. This principle was embodied in an Act of 1662 which authorized the levying of a capital sum or an annual rent in respect of the 'melioration' of property following street widenings in London. There were similar provisions in the Acts providing for the rebuilding of London after the Great Fire. The principle was revived and extended in the Planning Acts of 1909 and 1932. These allowed a local authority to claim, first 50 per cent, and then (in the later Act) 75 per cent, of the amount by which any property increased in value as the result of the operation of a planning scheme.

In fact these provisions were largely ineffective since it proved extremely difficult to determine with any uncertainty which properties had increased in value as a result of a scheme (or of works carried out under a scheme) or, where there was a reasonable degree of certainty, how much of the increase in value was directly attributable to the scheme and how much to other factors. The Uthwatt Committee, after reviewing previous experience, concluded:

No scheme has yet been devised under which in actual practice compensation and betterment can be equated in this way. In ascertaining the betterment there immediately arises the difficulty of establishing the amount by which a particular parcel of land has increased in value as the direct consequence of the restriction imposed on the other land and not from other causes. The shift of value resulting from the restriction may be to land which already possessed some building value; it may be to land hitherto of purely agricultural value; it may in part attach to land already built on; it may be to land nearby or to land far away. And, in any event, the increase is only an expectation value which may not materialize for years and in some cases will not materialize at all. Other influences may operate later and effect further shifts of values; and by the time a given site is finally developed and the owner reaps the increased value, innumerable factors may have intervened.

To the Uthwatt Committee the solution to these problems lay in changing the system of land ownership under which land had a development value dependent upon the prospects of its profitable use. They maintained that no new code for the assessment of compensation or the collection of betterment would be adequate if this individualistic system remained. The system itself had inherent 'contradictions provoking a conflict between private and public interest and hindering the proper operation of the planning machinery'. A new system was needed which would avoid these contradictions and which so unified existing rights in land as to 'enable shifts of value to operate within the same ownership'. The logic of this line of reasoning led to a consideration of land nationalization, but this the Committee rejected on the grounds that it would arouse keen political controversy, would involve probably insuperable financial problems, and would necessitate the establishment of a complicated national administrative machinery. In their view the solution to the problem lay in the nationalization not of land itself, but of all development rights in undeveloped land.

158

THE 1947 SCHEME

This, in essence, is the system which was introduced in 1947 and which still remains in operation, though it has been subject to major changes consequent upon the rise and fall of Governments.

The Town and Country Planning Act of 1947 nationalized all development rights, together with their associated values. Since the coming into operation of that Act, no development has been possible without the planning permission of the local authority. Development is defined as 'the carrying out of building, engineering, mining or other operations in, on, over or under land, or the making of any material change in the use of any buildings or other land'. This comprehensive definition is extended both by the legislation itself and by Orders made by the responsible Minister under its provisions. Though certain types of 'development' are specifically exempt, control extends over an extremely wide field: from city centre redevelopment to the change of a private residence to a boarding house.[5]

This development control system has weathered the political storms which have beset the compensation scheme which originally accompanied it. In brief, the 1947 Act nationalized development values and established a £300 million fund from which 'payments' were to be made (in 1953) to owners who could successfully claim that their land had some development value on the 'appointed day'— the day on which land owners could no longer realize their development values. As a result landowners now owned only the 'existing-use value' of their land. It followed that, if permission to develop were refused, no compensation was payable, and that when land was compulsorily purchased by public authorities the price was existing-use value.

If permission was given for development, a betterment levy ('development charge') was made. This was equivalent to the difference between the value of the land in its existing use and its value in the use for which the permission was granted.

In short, all development values were now vested in the State and anyone given a 'licence' to undertake development had to purchase them from the State by way of the development charge.

The underlying theory was that all land transactions would take place at existing-use values: there would be no incentive for anyone to pay more since the whole of the difference between the existing-use value and the market value would be taken by the development charge. However, in order to prevent sales at prices above existing use value, the Central Land Board (the body set up to administer

159

the whole scheme) was given power to buy land compulsorily—at the 'correct' price.

In retrospect it is clear that the decision to exact a development charge equal to the whole of the development value was misconceived. It was initially intended that a variable rate—less than 100 per cent—would be levied, but the Labour Government of the day maintained that 'the owner of land can have no possible claim to any part of the development value and it is logical and right that the State should, where development takes place, make a charge which represents the amount of the development value'.[6]

It may well have been logical but it produced difficulties, and these were increased by the reluctance of the Central Land Board to use its powers of compulsory purchase. The 100 per cent development charge removed all incentive to owners to sell land, and as a result, transactions took place at prices in excess of the existing use value.

The complexities of the scheme, the lack of public understanding and support, and—following the return of the Conservative Government in 1951 (one of whose first actions was to change the name of the Ministry of Local Government and Planning to the Ministry of Housing and Local Government)—the change in political emphasis from 'planning' to 'housing' (with a greatly expanded private sector): all these, as well as other factors (including fears about the economic impact of paying out the £300 million), led to the abandonment of the scheme.

There were alternatives which could have obviated the difficulties of the 1947 scheme. Greater resort could have been had to compulsory purchase at existing use value or the development charge could have been reduced to 75 per cent, 50 per cent or some other fraction of the development value. Neither of these alternatives was politically attractive to the Government of the day. Nevertheless, the nationalization of development *rights* was retained. Moreover, though a free market in private sales was restored, compulsory acquisition by public authorities remained on the basis of existing use values. Finally, though the £300 million fund was abolished, compensation for loss of development rights (up to 1947) was retained for 'admitted claims' under the 1947 scheme, but was payable only in certain defined cases and only at the point at which the owner actually suffered loss.

In the barest outline, this was the situation which obtained between 1953/54 and 1959. In the latter year, market value was restored for compulsory acquisition. Thus the dual market (one for private transactions and one for compulsory acquisitions by public authorities) established in 1954 was abolished and all land transactions

160

took place at 'market value'. But market value was, in fact, far removed from the concept familiar to theoretical economics. Indeed, to a large extent it was (and still is) determined by planning policies and decisions. Perhaps the clearest illustration of this is provided by comparing the situation of two owners of agricultural land, one piece of which is situated in an area zoned for development, while the other is situated in an adjacent green belt area which is 'protected' from development. The first benefits from the full value of his site for the use allowed by the local planning authority, but the second can realize only the existing-use value of his land. No question of compensation for the latter arises since all development rights belong to the State, though in the case of the first owner these have been given back to him without payment.

The price at which the first owner can sell his land will be dependent not only on demand but also on the use (including the density of development) which is allowed. But it may also be affected by planning decisions on other land. Indeed, the refusal of planning permission for development on the second piece of land referred to above, might well significantly enhance the 'market price' of the first piece.

Furthermore, planning policies can (and do) change. Green belts are not sacrosanct, and increasing pressures for more land can result in the 'release' of land for development which had previously been 'safe-guarded'. A Ministry concerned with increasing the output of new housing may well be more inclined to allow housing development than a local planning authority: an appeal to the Minister can result in permission being granted for an application which has been refused by a local authority. (In 1970, one-fifth of planning appeals in connection with new residential development were allowed by the Ministry.') [7]

THE LAND COMMISSION

A further attempt to provide a solution to this problem was made by the 1964–1970 Labour Government in the Land Commission Act of 1967, though this had an even shorter life than the 1947 scheme.

Briefly, the 1967 Act established a Land Commission which was to implement the 'two main objectives of the Government's land policy':

(i) to secure that the right land is available at the right time for implementation of national, regional and local plans;

(ii) to secure that a substantial part of the development value created by the community returns to the community and that the burden of the cost of land for essential purposes is reduced.[8]

It will be noted that the second of these objectives itself contained the seeds of a policy conflict: which was to predominate—the recoupment of development values or the reduction in the cost of land? Little was heard of the latter: it was the former which was easier to deal with. Benefiting from the experience of the 1947 scheme, the Act provided for a variable rate of betterment levy. Initially at 40 per cent of the development value it was to be increased to 45 per cent and then to 50 per cent 'at reasonably short intervals'. In fact it never was, but the object was to encourage land owners to sell: if they waited they might face a higher levy. This, however, ignored the wider political framework: owners could wait until the return of a Conservative Government which could implement its promise (as it did) to 'sweep it away into the junkheap where it belongs'.

The proceeds of the betterment levy were expected to amount to £80 million in a full year. There were, however, transitional arrangements and exemptions which resulted in a slow start. In 1968–69 some £15 million was levied and in 1969–70, £31 million. The following year was, of course, affected by the new Government's official statement that it intended to abolish the Commission: the amount levied rose only to £33 million.

It is not easy to assess the impact which the Commission had on facilitating the supply of land for development. They had strong powers of compulsory acquisition 'to ensure that the right land is made available at the right time', but they had to work within the framework of the existing planning system. Indeed, the original in-intention was that the Commission would work harmoniously with local planning authorities. But while Britain has a very sophisticated planning system, it is one designed to *control* land use rather than to *promote* the development of land. The Commission's role was supplementary to this: to ensure that land allocated for development was, in fact, developed. This they could do by using their powers of compulsory purchase to amalgamate land which was in separate ownerships; to acquire land whose owners could not be traced; and to purchase from owners who refused to sell or from builders who wished to retain land for future development.

The assumption was that sufficient land for development was being allocated by local planning authorities and that the role of the Commission was to effect its 'supply' into the market. It was rapidly found that this was not the case. In their first annual report, the Commission gently referred to the importance of their role in acting 'as a spur to those local planning authorities whose plans have not kept up with the demand for various kinds of development'. In their second report, a more forceful line was evident: they pointed to the inadequacy of the rate at which land was being released by local authorities. Exhortation by Ministers and by the Commission was proving inadequate. The Commission, therefore, began to act independently of (instead of 'harmoniously with') local authorities: they began to seek out land suitable for development and to apply for planning permission which, if refused, would have been subject to an appeal to the Minister.

This more positive approach was given insufficient time to make its effect. Though it was not abolished until 1971, its death was certain on 18 June 1970 (election day), and thereafter its activities were rapidly run down. Thus two major attempts to provide a comprehensive solution to the problems of compensation and betterment have come to grief (though the capital gains tax introduced in the 1967 Finance Act has been retained). But the problems remain: how far are they beyond the reach of those concerned with the art of the possible?

It is first necessary to be clear on what the problems are. These can be summarized under three headings: betterment, planning and the market and land supply.

BETTERMENT

Originally, the concept of betterment related to increases in site values resulting from public improvements such as road widenings, drainage or the provision of bridges and parks. Palgrave's *Dictionary of Political Economy* defined the principle of betterment as being 'that persons benefited by public expenditure should contribute to such expenditure to the extent of the increased value of their property, and thus not only if the improvement affected by the public authority was carried out for the purpose of conferring a benefit on such property, but also if the resulting benefit was purely accidental, the expenditure having been undertaken for a totally different purpose'.[9]

The concept was broadened, however, when it came to be related to general rises in site values consequent upon population increase, and economic and urban growth—as it was in the writings of Henry George for example. It was broadened in a different way when (under the first Planning Act in 1909) it was related to any increases in value caused 'by the making of any town planning scheme'.

At one extreme, therefore, betterment relates to the increases in value created by a specific public improvement, while at the other it relates to increases in value which result from much more general community actions or even economic growth. The common denominator is the fact that the increases in value, so far as the individual owner is concerned, are 'unearned'. They are created by external forces.

Some part of betterment is, of course, collected by the rating system, while capital gains tax recoups some of the profits on land transactions. The essence of the political question, however, is whether such taxes go far enough. Labour and Conservative Administrations have answered the question very differently.

The justification for going further is more than a judgement that 'the community' should benefit from the land values which it has collectively created. The value which attaches to any particular piece of land is so significantly affected by planning decisions that, to quote one experienced planner, 'planning authorities and their officials are in practice disturbing large amounts of income and wealth. This introduces tensions into planning practice. Planning aims are distorted in attempts to be fair as between owners, in allowing even densities, for example, on land with differing potential; and those whose income and wealth can be affected by the stroke of the drawing pen or drafting of a permission naturally tend to exert pressure so that there is always the possibility of graft in various forms.'[10]

Moreover, in their extensive land purchases for housing, schools, roads and other public services, public authorities must pay the full market values which they, themselves, have done so much to create.

To the extent that the issue is one of taxation it goes far beyond the scope of this book,[11] as does a consideration of the contemporary relevance of the 'logical solution' of land nationalization discussed (but rejected) by the Uthwatt Committee in 1942.[12] Where the issue becomes of further immediate relevance, however, is in relation to the British planning system and current problems of land supply.

PLANNING AND THE MARKET

The Uthwatt Committee proposed a solution to the compensation-betterment problem which attempted 'largely to preserve, in a highly developed economy, the purely individualistic approach to land ownership'. Their solution included an annual betterment levy on developed land (at a proposed rate of 75 per cent of the increase in value), compulsory acquisition (at 1939 values) of developed land required for redevelopment and, in respect of undeveloped land, State purchase of land needed for development, followed by a lease of the land to developers for an appropriate term at an appropriate charge.

The scheme amounted to a gradual nationalization of land (for which reason it was strongly opposed by Conservatives and welcomed by the Labour Party). Of particular note is the strong emphasis which was placed on public acquisition of land prior to development or redevelopment. This emphasis was lacking in the operation of both the 1947 and 1967 Acts and (at least on one interpretation) was responsible for their failure. Since owners had no incentive to sell, compulsory acquisition was necessary. The alternative was to leave some proportion of the development value to the owners. Either scheme would have worked. What was unworkable was a scheme (as in the 1947 Act) under which there was neither an incentive to sell nor sufficient compulsory acquisition to maintain the required supply of land.

Nevertheless, whether workable or not, both the Uthwatt proposals and the 1947 Act constituted a 'once and for all' solution. The 'market' for land was entirely replaced by a State system. This logically followed from the nationalization of development rights.

The abandonment of the 1947 scheme led to an uneasy marriage between a non-market 'planning' solution and a market solution. This is the situation today, following the similar abandonment of the 1967 scheme. Development rights belong to the community, but the associated development values run with planning permission.

What, it must be asked, is the function of the market in this situation? Since the planning machine determines land use, the market operates only to allocate particular permitted land uses to specific purchasers. This is the justification for the suggestion that development rights might be sold by auction.[13] It is also the justification for all developers (public as well as private) paying the full 'market price' for land in the use which is allocated to it by the local planning authority.

The alternative is to abandon market influences entirely: as would be done if land were nationalized and allocated (to individual developers) entirely by administrative decisions. Despite the shortcomings of the present British situation, there can be few who would argue in support of this alternative.

A simple economic principle should not, however, be forgotten.

165

The market price is a function of both demand and supply. If 'insufficient' land is made available, the price will rise. Nevertheless, the issue is complicated by the fact that land supply is in the control of two independent parties—the owner of the land and the local planning authority. By refusing to sell, or by refusing to zone land for development, either one or both parties can (quite independently and for very different reasons) hold up the supply of potentially developable land.

LAND SUPPLY

The total 'supply' of land is, for all practical purposes, fixed; but, given the extensive system of land use control in Britain, the actual supply of land for development is determined by local planning authorities. If this supply is inadequate to meet current demands its price will rise. This has undoubtedly happened in recent years. Statistics are hard to come by, but Tables 40 and 41 are illustrative. Between 1966 and 1970, housing plot prices rose by 50 per cent in England and Wales. Greater increases took place in the areas of high

Table 40   *Land Price Index and Private Sector Housing Land, 1963–1971**

Price per plot (1966 = 100)

	North	Midlands & Wales	South (excluding Greater London)	Greater London	England & Wales
1963	67	58	77	82	74
1964	77	78	89	84	84
1965	88	91	96	92	94
1966	100	100	100	100	100
1967	102	97	106	95	102
1968	113	110	125	106	118
1969	176	125	152	123	147
1970	137	153	157	128	150
1971 (1st half)					169

* *Housing Statistics, Great Britain*, No. 23, November 1971, p. 75. The table gives indices of weighted average prices per plot of housing land. The weights are fixed and chosen so that the indices measure the price of a standard collection of parcels of land, similar to those developed around 1966. Land prices are very variable, and this leads to difficulties in constructing price indices. The indices do provide a guide to trends in prices, but they cannot be taken as being precise. This applies particularly to the regional indices. Details of the construction of the indices and further information on land prices can be found in an article 'An Index of Housing Land Prices', *Economic Trends*, No. 208, February 1971.

166

demand, particularly in the Midlands and Southern England. As a proportion of the price of a new house, the cost of land rose from 11·9 per cent in 1963 to between 16·3 and 18 per cent in the third quarter of 1971. While average new house prices over this period rose by 85 per cent, the increase in the price of an unserviced plot rose by 152–179 per cent.

It is this increase which has again brought the question of betterment to the fore, though the current Government response is to stress the importance of land supply. Logically, this is correct. The high prices are a *symptom* of shortage in relation to effective demand. A comprehensive system for the recoupment of betterment would not affect this—though it is desirable for reasons of equity. Indeed, shortages can rarely be satisfactorily dealt with by 'controls' (hence the war-time 'black market'). If land prices for new housing were controlled, the shortage would be reflected in increased profits for builders or high re-sale prices.

The recent increases in land prices (in some areas) have been so great as to lead to the curious situation that it is more profitable for an owner to hold on to his land (allowing it to appreciate in value) rather than release it for development. How far this is a significant factor, it is impossible to say. And now that the Land Commission has been abolished there is no machinery ready to hand to ensure that 'available' land is developed.

Table 41   *Relationship Between Unserviced Land Prices and New House Prices in England and Wales, 1963–1971* [14]

	Average price per unserviced plot £s	Average new house price £s	Land price as % of house selling price
1963	377	3,195	11·9
1964	434	3,433	12·6
1965	485	3,768	12·9
1966	517	4,030	12·8
1967	527	4,283	12·3
1968	610	4,499	13·6
1969	760	4,819	15·8
1970	775	5,128	15·1
1971 (third quarter)	950 to 1,050	5,897	16·3 to 18·0
% Increase 1963–1971	152–779%	85%	

THE 1972 LAND SHORTAGE

This brief discussion highlights some of the major elements in land policy. Given a restrictionist land policy, increased land values give

167

rise to large profits on the sale of land. The planning machine effect-ively reduces the supply and thus increases these profits (and, of course, the cost to public authorities of acquiring land for public authority housing, schools and other services). Yet, increased supply can be brought about only by a less restrictionist policy.

At the time of writing (April 1972), considerable concern is caused by the inflation of housing and housing-land prices. As is usual in such situations, 'Conservative governments tend to blame narrow-minded local authorities and Labour governments to blame greedy private speculators'.[15] The phase is probably a temporary one—precipitated by such factors as a rise in earnings during 1969 and 1970 which was not accompanied by parallel increase in house prices; by a marked fall in house building in these years; and by the current increase in the availability of funds for mortgages.

The Minister for Local Government and Development is re-ported [16] to be considering a streamlining of planning procedures and radically changing the system of planning control which has been in operation since 1948: instead of applying for planning per-mission, developers would simply register their 'intention to develop' and it would be incumbent upon local planning authorities to take positive action to prevent development if they considered it to be undesirable.

There are obvious dangers in commenting on current debates: the time lag between writing and publication gives the reader the advan-tage of being able to check the comments against what has happened in the meantime. Nevertheless, the current proposals have all the appearance of a round in the game of bluff which so frequently char-acterises central–local government relationships.

The target is, of course, a false one. It is not planning procedures which are at fault (though this is not to say that they cannot be improved). The basic problem is that of adjusting supply to demand. It may be true that 'land is in short supply because owners, realizing that they have an appreciating asset, are either asking a very high price or are holding on to their assets in hope of a further apprecia-tion'—as is maintained by the planners.[17] It may be equally true that local authorities are being tardy in releasing land—as is main-tained by developers. It is also likely that there is some truth in both contentions and also that suitable land cannot be released because (in response to previous Government restrictions) it lacks water and sewage disposal services. One useful idea which emerges from the debate is the proposal for a 'Domesday Book' of all land owned by public authorities: but why not land owned by private developers as well? This again was one of the functions which the Land Commission was particularly well-suited to fulfil. Much of the heat emanating from the current controversy could be removed by the publication of the facts of the situation.

This excursion into the immediately topical scene is likely to be of only passing interest. Indeed, the indications are that the issue is a purely temporary one, except in certain 'pressure areas' where there is a long-term clash between effective demand and planning policies. (There will always be a demand for housing in the London green belt: this cannot be met except by abandoning much of the green belt policy.)

THE PLANNING FAILURE

Time will show how true (or wide of the mark) these comments are. More important for the current discussion is the planning failure which is highlighted. The British planning system is much better geared to prevention than it is to promotion. It tends to allocate land at a rate which is inadequate to meet demand and this forces up prices. It needs to be remembered that the system was designed a quarter of a century ago when assumptions concerning population and economic growth, mobility and land demands were made which have been since proved false. The system has yet to come to terms with the affluent society.

Nevertheless, an affluent society has the wealth to protect, conserve and enhance environmental values. This inevitably reduces the supply of land available for development in key locations and (to the extent that demand cannot be equally well met elsewhere) results in rising land values. Whatever revisions are needed in planning policy (some suggestions on urban growth policy have been made in an earlier chapter) major restrictions are both necessary and desirable. Put thus, a different issue emerges: who is to pay? Here we enter into the relatively uncharted field of the distribution of benefits and costs brought about by the planning system. Professor Lichfield has developed an extremely useful tool of analysis with the 'Planning Balance Sheet',[18] but this does not (and does not pretend to) attempt to follow through all the social implications of planning policies. The type of question raised in the *Observations on the Greater London Development Plan* by the Centre for Environmental Studies (reproduced in Volume III) do not lend themselves easily to analysis. They are, nevertheless, important questions and research is urgently needed which will combine the advantages of Professor Lichfield's approach with those of the sociologist.

The narrower problem of land values is also complex, and any solution demands the support of a well-informed electorate. Much of the failure of post-war policy in this field has been caused in part by a lack of public understanding, debate and support. The increasing public concern for 'the environment' and new thinking on citizen-participation (to which we return in the final chapter of Volume II) offer hope that a political basis may emerge for a third attempt to deal with the problems of land values.

References and Further Reading

1. There is inevitably some overlap between this chapter and the chapter on 'Planning and Land values' in the author's *Town and Country Planning in Britain*, Allen & Unwin, 4th edition, 1972. The latter, however, deals rather more fully with the various post-war legislative attempts to 'solve' the compensation problem, while the present chapter is more discursive and discusses current problems more fully.

2. The qualifications which are needed to this statement need not concern us in this brief account (e.g. certain requirements could be imposed in the interests of what was termed 'good neighbourliness': these were not compensatable). For a lucid account of 'The History of Compensation and Betterment Since 1900' by H. R. Parker see Chapter 4 of P. Hall (ed.), *Land Values*, Sweet & Maxwell, 1965.

3. This and other quotations are from the Uthwatt Report: *Report of the Expert Committee on Compensation and Betterment*, Cmd. 6398, HMSO, 1942.

4. C. M. Haar, *Land Planning Law in a Free Society*, Harvard University Press, 1951, p. 99.

5. For a fuller non-technical exposition, see *Town and Country Planning in Britain*, op. cit., Chapter IV. More detail is given in D. Heap, *An Outline of Planning Law*, Sweet & Maxwell, 5th edition, 1969; and in D. Heap, *Encyclopedia of the Law of Town and Country Planning*, Sweet & Maxwell, 1959, and periodic supplements.

6. *H. C. Debates*, Vol. 451, 26 May 1948.

7. Department of the Environment, *Handbook of Statistics 1970*, HMSO, 1971, Table 28.

8. White Paper, *The Land Commission*, Cmnd. 2771, HMSO, 1965.

9. Quoted in the Uthwatt Report, *Final Report of the Expert Committee on Compensation and Betterment*, Cmd. 6386, HMSO, 1942, p. 104.

10. N. Lichfield, 'Land Nationalisation' in P. Hall (ed.), *Land Values*, op. cit., p. 110.

11. For further discussion see Uthwatt Report, op. cit.; P. Hall (ed.), *Land Values*, op. cit.; R. Turvey, *The Economics of Real Property*, Allen & Unwin, 1957; F. G. Pennance, *Housing, Town Planning and the Land Commission*, Insitute of Economic Affairs, 1967; and D. R. Denman, *Land in the Market*, Institute of Economic Affairs, 1964.

12. See N. Lichfield, op. cit.

13. F. G. Pennance, *Housing, Town Planning and the Land Commission*, Institute of Economic Affairs, 1967.

14. *Building Societies Gazette*, March 1972, p. 229.

15. 'Land at any Price', *The Economist*, 8 April 1972, p. 24.

16. *The Times*, 13 April 1972.

17. See letter from the President of the Royal Town Planning Institute to *The Times*, 18 April 1972.

18. See, for example, N. Lichfield, 'Cost Benefit Analysis in Urban Expansion: A Case Study: Peterborough', *Regional Studies*, Vol. 3, 1969, pp. 123–155; N. Lichfield and H. Chapman, 'Cost Benefit Analysis in Urban Expansion: A Case Study: Ipswich', *Urban Studies*, Vol. 7, 1970, pp. 156–179; N. Lichfield and H. Chapman, 'Cost Benefit Analysis and Road Proposals for a Shopping Centre: A Case Study: Edgware', *Journal of Transport Economics and Policy*, Vol. 2, 1968, pp. 280–320; and N. Lichfield and H. Chapman, 'Financial Analysis' in G. Ashworth, 'Environmental Recovery at Skelmersdale', *Town Planning Review*, Vol. 41, 1970, pp. 282–287.

Index